Stories of ROOTWORKERS & HOODOO *in the Mid-South*

Stories of ROOTWORKERS & HOODOO *in the Mid-South*

TONY KAIL

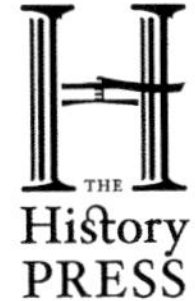

Published by The History Press
Charleston, SC
www.historypress.com

Front cover, top left: courtesy of author's collection; *top center*: courtesy of Farm Security Administration—Office of War Information Photograph Collection. Library of Congress; *top right*: courtesy of author's collection; *bottom*: courtesy of Shelby County Library. *Back cover, left*: courtesy of author's collection; *right*: courtesy of author's collection.

First published 2019

Manufactured in the United States

ISBN 9781467139892

Library of Congress Control Number: 2019945092

CONTENTS

ACKNOWLEDGEMENTS

There are a number of folklorists, historians, practitioners, families and scholars to whom I am extremely grateful, including the following: Jack Montgomery; Yvonne Chireau; Jeffrey Anderson; Carolyn Morrow Long; Katrina Hazzard-Donald; Robert Farris Thompson; David Metcalfe; Judith McWillie; Bill Ferris; Dorothy Armour; P.D. Newman; Miss Jessie, Terry Saunders and A. Schwab, Elliot Schwab; Debbie Halstead and Ebbo, Lucky Heart Cosmetics; Keystone Laboratories; Shelby County Public Library, Memphis; Cleveland Public Library; Doc Macon and the Macon family; Mother Jones, Lisa and Memphis Conjure; Bernice Strickland and the Strickland family; Madam Glover and the Glover family; Dr. Charles Champion and family; Bill Steber; Michael Pascoe; Miller's Rexall; and my best friend and wife, Amy

INTRODUCTION

10:00 p.m., October 22, 1934
Jackson, Mississippi

The light from Police Chief Simmons's flashlight cut through the darkness like a knife. The yellow-tinted beam of light was filled with dancing dust as it pierced the darkened dirt path into the woods. Lush green plants and spiraling kudzu covered the path, creating a tunnel effect into the property. Two officers followed Simmons as they crushed fallen branches and snapping twigs on the ground under their black leather boots. The Mississippi heat beat down on the men, sending trails of salty sweat down their foreheads. The trail seemed to go on forever, until the chief spotted tiny starlike flames through the darkness.

The humidity seemed to push the officers' uniforms against their flesh as their hearts began to race. The two men seemed lost as they followed the chief into the darkness. It was only a few hours ago that he had told them of this "special operation." The chief remained silent regarding the reason for this raid. He knew that if he mentioned the word *voodoo* it might affect the operation. Voodoo was a mystical phenomenon that was practiced in the back fields of farms among the impoverished black families, Simmons assumed. The curious chief had recently been alerted by a local informant that there was some sort of voodoo operation going on in an abandoned farm near the river.

The sparkling lights that danced in the darkness appeared to be getting clearer as the hushed sound of voices could be heard in the thicket ahead. The men could make out the shape of an old house made of rotting wood. Simmons turned to his men and raised his finger to his lips as an eerie voice cried out from within the structure: "And the Holy Ghost is gonna take that spirit. Ohhhhh Lord, that spirit has no place in this man. Take it out!" The booming voice drowned out the sound of insects chirping in the night sky. Simmons's hand slid down and rested on the leather snap that held his revolver in the holster. "Pop!," the leather snap sounded as he removed the only thing holding back his weapon from being drawn. The sound of echoing pops from his officers soon followed.

As the men drew nearer, a scent of burning herbs that reminded the chief of his wife's cooking spices caused his nostrils to flare. The flames of candles could be seen illuminating through a chamois covering the window of the old wood house. The light from the candles grew as it cast a shadow on the walls, lighting shifting shapes of human figures. Chief Simmons could hear his officers' breathing grow ever more intense.

Simmons turned and whispered to the men, "There is no telling what we are about to see. Just follow my lead and make sure we round everyone up that's in this building." The men nodded as they wondered to themselves if this was going to be yet another bootlegging or prostitution operation.

As the men slowly walked out of the woods into the open yard before them, the light of the summer moon shined brightly, destroying any possibility of remaining hidden. The chief turned and raised his finger. "Let's go." The three officers rushed toward the wooden door as the chief reached down and twisted the doorknob. "Boom!" The door slammed against the wall of the house as Simmons's boot crashed into the door. "Everybody freeze!" he yelled. "Police!"

Clouds of flowing white smoke filled the room as silhouettes of men and women fell to the floor. Simmons's eyes began to run along the walls of the room decorated with crosses and pictures of Jesus and saints. A table filled with various burning colored candles lit the room. Bowls of dried plants and glass bottles filled with multicolored oils adorned a wooden table in the corner.

As one of the younger officers began to walk toward a door on the east side of the room, he noticed the threshold of the room changing colors. Swinging his sidearm into the door, the officer's eyes widened as a revolving colored lamp sat in the corner. An elderly man was in the corner, staring at the floor under a dark colored statue that held a burning bowl of incense. A

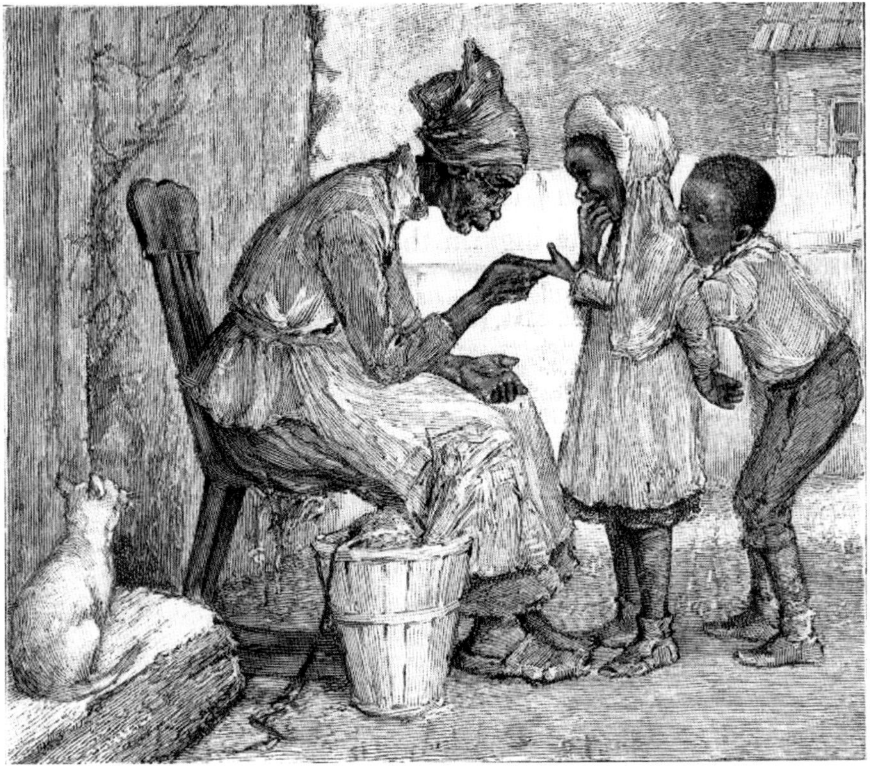

Courtesy of New York Public Library.

young girl lay on a crude operating table against the far wall of the room. As frightened as she appeared to the officers, she would later go on to attest to the healing powers of the owner of this operation.

Doctor Claude Jones was arrested by Mississippi authorities for running a "hoodoo hospital" in the cradle of the Delta on Sunday October 21, 1934, in Jackson, Mississippi. As a spiritual doctor and rootworker specializing in African American healing practices, Jones created a clandestine spiritual sanctuary for local black men and women who struggled with sickness as well as spiritual curses. The local press described the activities of the hospital and Dr. Jones in tales of crystal balls, witchcraft and mystic potions. As usual, what actually went on in that facility was very different from what was reported in the outside press.

This would be one of the many discoveries of evidence of hoodoo and conjure in the Mid-South. There are several more, and these are their stories....

1
THE SECRET INSTITUTION

I must go with him to another part of the woods where there was a certain root, which if I would take some of it with me, carrying it always on my right side, would render it impossible for Mr. Covey or any other white man to whip me.
—*Frederick Douglass*

The practices of rootwork and conjure were born out of the healing and spiritual traditions of Africa. These rich traditions were kept alive in secret amid the abuse and violence of slavery. As slaves were brought into the Delta and families expanded through the Mid-South, the practices that aided in their survival began to pour over into the public's eye. What was once hidden in plain sight was being observed by outsiders, who, in most cases, ridiculed and shunned the practices, while a segment of nonpractitioners feared, respected and sometimes even used these traditions.

The culture of hoodoo was so prolific throughout African American communities throughout the United States that its practices even garnered the attention of the president of the United States. In 1919, Woodrow Wilson stood before Congress, and as he was reaching into his pocket, he accidentally dropped a piece of red cloth. The president explained to the members of Congress and the press that he had dropped his "conjure bag" and that he kept it to help his rheumatism and other problems. Wilson chuckled, as did the members of Congress. While the concept of the "conjure bag" was being laughed at, it also became apparent that hoodoo had made quite an impact on the consciousness of the country. The once-secret institution of healing and magic was no longer a secret.

As the practices of Africa and African Americans began to be revealed in southern society, they also continued to be feared and demeaned. Reactions found in Mid-South newspapers from Kentucky, Mississippi and Tennessee and carried in other papers nationwide starting in the early 1920s were quite alarming:

> *Hoodoos or African Witches are operating in Boyle County with frightful results. Seven colored citizens have already been driven to the mad house by the alleged satanic influences of the hoodoos.* [*Kentucky Advocate* (Danville, KY), May 7, 1925]

> *Devil Worship still exists. Voodoo Practices Originating in Africa, Have Not Lost Their Hold Among Negroes in America. The witch doctor business thrives among the Negroes of the South and to some extent to the North. It is a kind of magical art called Voodoo and came originally from Africa. For a moderate price you can buy a "hoohoo" packet from a voodoo woman that is guaranteed if fastened to his front gate inconspicuously to cause your enemy to sicken and die. It contains such articles as bits of bone, a tooth or two feathers.* [*Cuba (KS) Daylight*, March 21, 1918]

> *Rumblings of African mumbo-jumbo were heard in the juvenile court as a delegation of Negroes came here from Athens Tennessee to protest holding of a negro girl named Susie. The delegation told Judge L.D. Miller that Susie paroled from the state training school recently was "doing well" and that charges against her were "conjured up by dat ol' hoodoo."* [*Corpus Christi (TX) Caller-Times*, August 27, 1937]

The practice of traditional healing and conjure was frequently looked on as foolish superstition by those outside of the African American community in the Mid-South. Traditional practices that had been performed for years were often mocked in the public eye. Newspapers sharing reports of African American folk practices would typically describe them in a condescending and racist manner. A 1906 news story in the *Natchez Democrat* out of Natchez, Mississippi, shared the sentiments of many white southerners at the time. The article, "Forty Years of Freedom: Negroes Retain the Foolish Idea as to the Power of the Conjure Bag," said:

> *Mr. Austin Smith, owner of Saragrossa plantation, this county, drove into the city wearing a most amused smile on his always beaming face and when questioned as to the whenceness and whereof for the smile, he said "Forty years of freedom have not been enough to eradicate the idea from the negro's mind that the conjure bag is the only thing that will keep the witches off, or break a hoodoo." Saying this he extracted from his pocket a conjure bag that one of the negroes on his place had dropped. It was a red flannel concern, wrapped with seven pieces of string and contained a piece of silver, a bit of graveyard dust, a piece of lodestone and some hair from a graveyard rabbit's leg. The string was wrapped around the bag so that it left a long loop over the wrist, and the owner of the bag would hold the bag in the hand while shaking hands with the person they wish to conjure. In case of driving witches away from the house the negroes wave the bag above the head* [and] *indulge in some kind of monologue that is beyond understanding.*

News of the "pagan practices" of African folk healing and culture became a popular topic among members of the wealthy upper class. Traditions were viewed as "devilish" and at the same time "exotic" to those outside of the culture. Newspapers in northern states ran articles about the "Southern Negro" who participated in "wild" African rituals. Following a high-profile incident in Montgomery, Alabama, involving a member of an African healing culture, the *Montgomery Advertiser* spoke of how "a shabby, smelly room on Montgomery's Monroe Street could just have easily been a thatched hut in the jungles of Haiti and the 'witch woman' who practiced her voodoo rites over a smelly brew could have readily been a sorceress of that Island of Black Magic."

In 1915, a group of politicians gathered in the Waldorf Astoria Hotel in New York to listen to an animated Tennessee judge named Benjamin Franklin Adams as he discussed southern culture. The conversation drifted into the topic of hoodoo and "conjure bags" in the South:

> *What I have noticed hereabout don't even know what I mean when I speak about a conjure-bag. A conjure-bag is like one of those things like potlicker and crackling-bread which can only be made by an expert. It is considered extremely efficacious among the colored population of our section of the country, and not a few of the poor whites pin their faith in it. If you put it where your enemy has to step over it, it will deprive him of the use of himself and you can bring upon him any kind of evil fortune. In the preparation of a conjure bag as well as its use. The strictest secrecy must*

always be observed. Should the intended victim discover it, he can convert it to his own uses by simply putting it into running water. The owner of the bag will then go crazy.

The judge went on to talk about the work of a rootworker in Brownsville, Tennessee, known as Aunt Phoebe Thompson. Aunt Phoebe was well known for making powerful mojo bags. The judge described to an interested audience the ingredients of local mojo bags in West Tennessee: "I should explain gentlemen that some of the ingredients that go toward the making of every real conjure bag besides those requisites I have mentioned a crow's foot, a snake bone, some yarn and string with has been dyed with some copperas, some game rooster blood and various other components of less importance, but still necessary."

RED 'CONJURE BAG' PRESIDENT'S JINX FOR RHEUMATISM

When the President arose to make his statement to his Congressional guests on Wednesday night, he accidentally pulled from his pocket a bit of red cloth, which fell to the floor.

He explained that he had dropped his conjure bag, used for the rheumatism and for other purposes. He laughed and the crowd laughed with him.

This put the entire audience in a fine frame of mind for the conference.

The prevalence of hoodoo throughout North America caught the attention of a U.S. president. Woodrow Wilson joked with Congress that he carried a "conjure" bag for his rheumatism. *Courtesy of* Washington Times.

While Hoodoo and African American folk practices were frequently mocked as foolishness by those outside of the black community, these practices were often perceived as posing a threat to communities.

For example, in 1908, a courtroom in Little Rock, Arkansas, became frozen in silence as a young black man stood before a jury. Louis Hursch had been brought in as a suspect in the murder of a local farmer. The farmer, Sam Haywood, had been called to his doorway by an unknown subject. When Haywood approached the threshold of his home, he was struck by a gunshot.

As the accused suspect, Louis Hursch stood quivering in front of the courtroom. The jury listened to his testimony, and as the court's proceedings came to an end, a member of the jury stood to his feet. The juror demanded that a test be performed on the murder weapon to ascertain if the gunman was indeed guilty. The African American jury member requested a "folk"

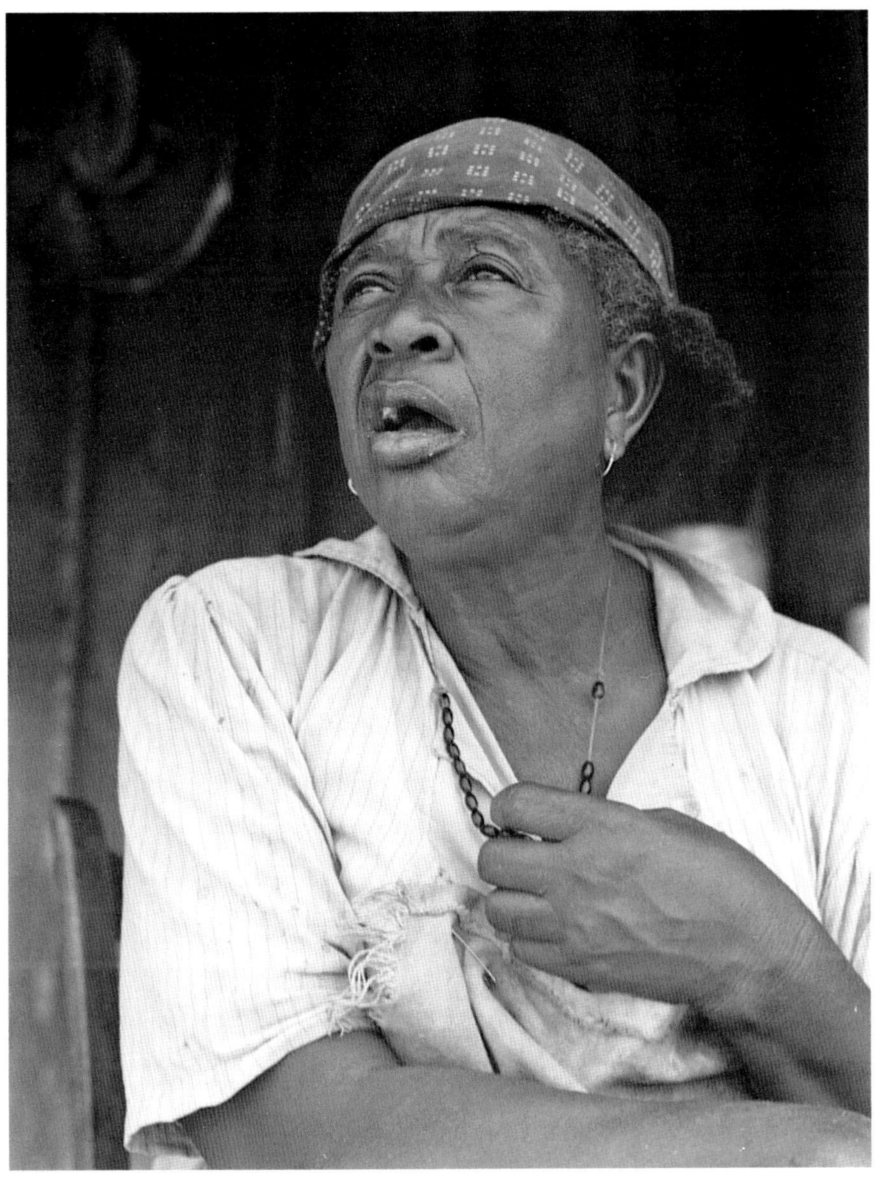

Evidence of early spiritual tools in the Mid-South. This 1937 photograph shows a Mississippi sharecropper wearing a black beaded necklace believed to protect against heart problems. *Courtesy of Farm Security Administration—Office of War Information Photograph Collection. Library of Congress.*

test that had become popular in the local black community. The court would run a "voodoo test" to see if the man was guilty. The test involved firing the weapon; any evidence of guilt would manifest in the form of blood on the barrel of the gun. The jury member claimed that a gun used to murder would "sweat blood at the muzzle." The gun was fired, and a strange red color was observed at the end of the gun's barrel. Upon seeing the appearance of the symbol of guilt, Hursch pulled out a knife and plunged it into his own throat. Unfortunately, the red residue on the gun was later determined to be rust.

THE HOODOO BOOGEYMAN

Many communities in the Mid-South were quite frightened of African American healing and spiritual cultures. This culminated from a mixture of racism, bias and fear stemming from myths about race and culture. Mythical stories and misinterpretations of religion that came out of New Orleans seemed to set the stage for the paranoia and fear of rootwork and conjure in the Mid-South. New Orleans was often looked on as the "mecca" of hoodoo, voodoo and African "pagan" practices. Media reports seldom accurately described the African diaspora in Louisiana, instead focusing on sensationalized reports of animal and human sacrifice, zombies and curses. The potential for African religion to bond its devotees was often feared by slave owners. In some cases, practitioners were punished for merely practicing traditions.

> *Fifteen Negro men and women were arrested in New Orleans last week for participating in the African Voudou dance. When taken they had images placed around the room as is the custom in Africa. They were ordered 50 lashes each. The dance is most obscene and brutal.*

This was not restricted to the Mid-South. A 1901 public report regarding lynchings in Illinois listed a number of crimes that had been punished by lynching, including murder, arson, rape and "voodooism."

National newspapers featured headlines such as "Secrets of Vicious Voodoo Doctors Who Victimize Gullible Girls." The "Voodoo Boogeyman" in the South was slowly created by stories like this one from an 1870 publication:

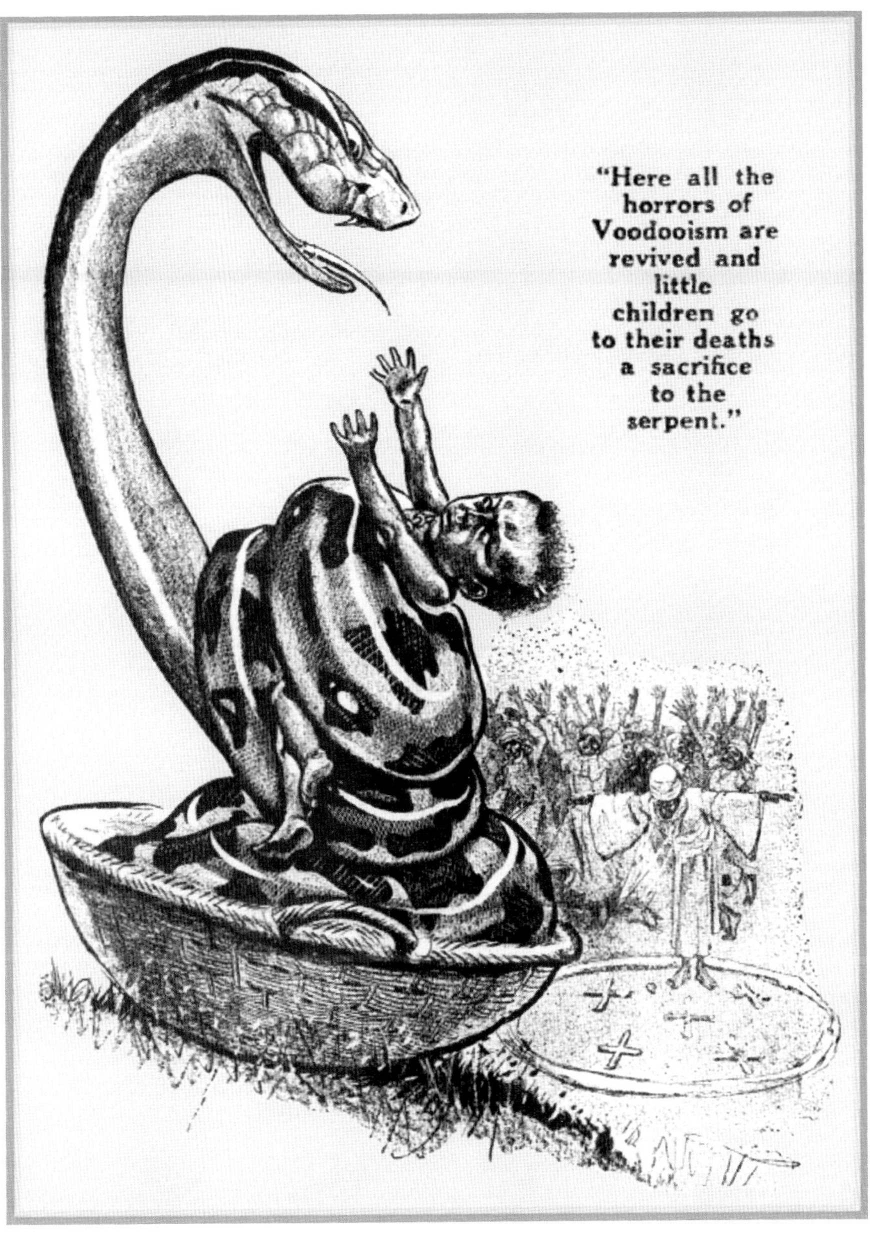

Newspapers across the United States carried stories about the presence of African-based cultures in the Mid-South as well as the many urban legends surrounding traditional cultures. *Courtesy of* El Paso Herald.

New Orleans is just now greatly excited over the sudden disappearance of a white infant child belonging to a Mr. Digby who is believed to have been stolen by a negro woman for the purpose of sacrifice on a voudou altar. Constant and unremitting search has been made without success, not withstanding heavy rewards have been offered for the recovery of the child. No one appears to feel authorized to say it was stolen for sacrificial purposes, yet the thousands believe such was the case of its abduction.

Legendary Vodou queen Marie Laveau became the ultimate "boogeywoman" as the Mid-South caught wind of stories about her from local and national media. Ominous headlines, like this one out of Nashville, Tennessee, in 1930 warned, "Black Shadows of Congo Gods Hover over

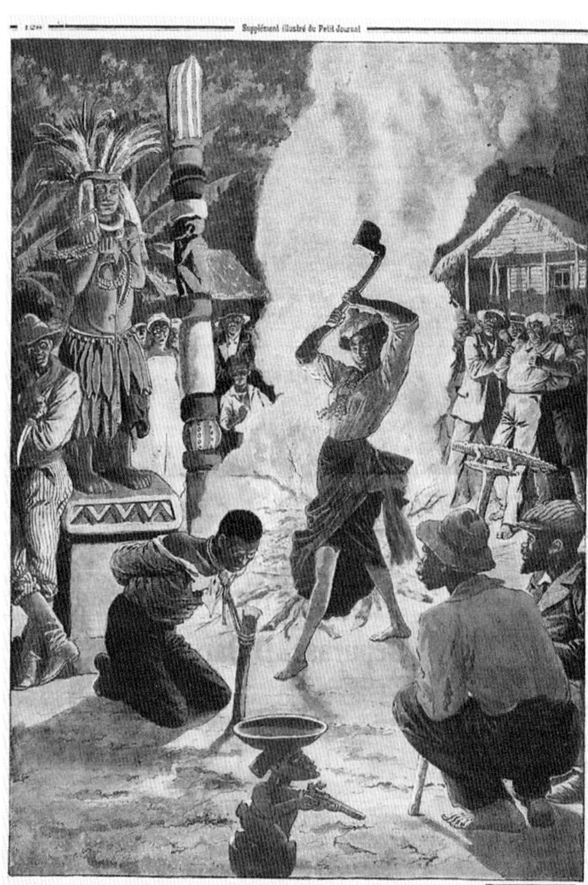

As a result of the large number of African traditions in New Orleans, many cities in the Mid-South feared that any evidence of African culture would turn their communities into similar entities. Most myths and legends surrounding New Orleans focused on tales of human sacrifice and black-magic rituals. *Courtesy of author's collection.*

Snug Cottage in New Orleans. Large Salt Cross, 'Gris-Gris', a Voodoo Curse Appears on Front Porch."

Reports of spiritual workers from the Mid-South who performed spiritual readings and healings in New Orleans brought about suspicion of these specialists importing destructive activities back into the Mid-South. In 1889, Mississippi-born spiritual healer James Alexander was arrested in New Orleans for disturbing the peace. Alexander was believed to have a spiritual power, as he was born with a caul or "veil" over his face that signified his special abilities. He was arrested as part of a party of men and women who were engaged in dancing and loud behavior. The spiritual healer told police that he was in the process of providing treatments for several clients as neighbors complained about the loud shouting coming from the building. Accounts tell of dancing, shouting, spiritual treatments and men and women dressed in loose clothing. Many of the same characteristics would be found in a number of the diverse African healing and spiritual traditions throughout the Mid-South.

As Mid-South communities began to see African folk practitioners as invading enemies, threats of violence began to rise with reports out of cities like Memphis of local citizens assaulting rootworkers. Law enforcement in cities like Memphis and Montgomery began a series of campaigns that included mass arrests, undercover operations and rounding up of spiritual workers in black communities. Lest it be thought that using terms like *war* are this author's personal description of these campaigns, it should be understood that this was the terminology used by communities and agencies engaged in these campaigns. Memphis newspapers ran headlines like "Voodooism Called Plain Racket by Warring Tennessee Police," while an Alabama newspaper announced, "Detective Wages War on Black Magic Here." It became very apparent that there was a definite agenda in the attack on African traditions.

Health Care and Rootwork

Rootworking practices were frequently met with dismissal and in some cases disdain by not only the law but also those in the medical field. African healing techniques in areas like Louisiana in the 1940s were blamed for the spread of diseases and hinderances to preventative care. Issues like the growth of syphilis in African American communities was blamed on indifference from the rootworking community. Spiritual healers were frequently referred to as "quacks" and "witch doctors." Louisiana state officials warned the outside community about African practices. A report from the Works Project Administration's (WPA) Venereal Disease Control Project warned: "We know of a number of instances in which negroes have paid from one to fifty dollars to voodoo doctors for charms to ward off evil spirits. In most instances, the charm better known to the victims of the voodoo doctors as the 'hand' usually consists of a bag filled with a concoction of crushed bone, peach seeds, frog stools and other ingredients. This bag they wear around the neck. Sometimes the treatment of the voodoo doctor is accompanied by chants in an unknown tongue and by dances and other primitive maneuvers." Along with ethnocentric descriptions like "primitive," health departments began to post signs and posters featuring images of rootworkers, warning the public of their "dangerous" practices. One particular poster featured a group of African American men sitting around a boiling cauldron while a "witch doctor" presided over a healing ceremony. The "witch doctor" in question was actually a local New Orleans healer who had been photographed preparing a mojo hand. The WPA would go on to have several interactions with African and African American spirituality, including the collection of testimonies of former slaves and their role in spiritual and healing cultures and the production of a federally funded version of Shakespeare's *Macbeth* that became known as "Voodoo Macbeth," featuring an all-black cast performing the Bard's classic set in Haiti and directed by none other than Orson Welles.

Medical professionals seemed to be either fascinated by the holistic methods of rootwork used to heal both physically and spiritually or appalled at the use of such works. Some professionals claimed to have patients who were undergoing stresses that were attributed to conjure. The 1949 death of a thirty-two-year-old African American female in Montgomery brought attention to cultural stresses and trauma as a possible result of conjure. The woman had discovered a number of strange objects around her home, including various cloths, feathers and colored vials of powder. She feared that someone had crossed her, and she had begun to panic. Over a period of five days, the woman began to grow physically ill. The following evening, she dropped dead. Her death certificate stated that she had died of an acute heart failure. However, the local press stated that "coroners, doctors and others who sign death certificates are somewhat loathe to sign their names to a certificate with the cause of death as Voodoo, Obeah, Wanga or other names for the

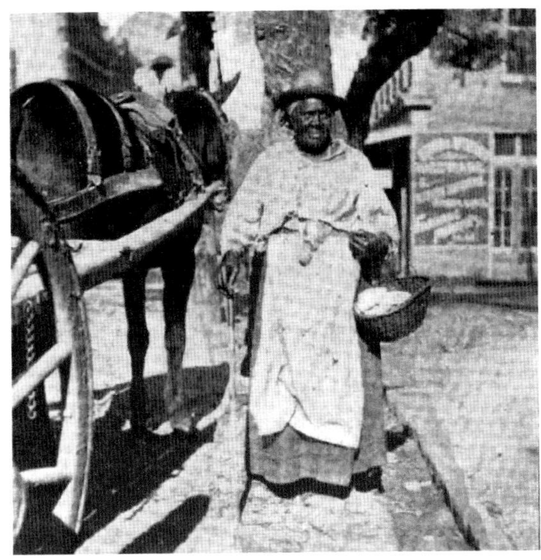

Some spiritual workers were labeled "witch doctors" by those outside the culture. Mam Liza was a Mississippi spiritual worker who worked on a plantation in the Delta. *Courtesy of* Frank Leslie's Popular Monthly, *Volume XLIV, July to December 1897.*

black art which has existed in the South since before the War Between the States." Alabama's state toxicologist, Dr. C.J. Rehling, had testified at a number of trials involving conjure. Rehling in his spare time began to collect a number of "fetishes," as they were called, including amulets made from animal remains and mojo bags. The toxicologist spoke on the effectiveness of conjure: "Voodoo can kill. There are of course many complex elements that contribute to such death: the degree of superstition of the victim, cardiac condition, the pitch of fear, imagination, fear of the unknown, some neurosis reflected in the physical condition, education and hysteria inclination."

Physicians in Tennessee and Mississippi were often critical of black spiritual healers in the Mid-South. Memphis-based physicians had been noted as criticizing the growth of spiritual healers on Beale Street and the loss of patients to rootworkers in the city. The Mississippi State Board of Health became so concerned about the popularity of African American spiritual doctors that they issued a public statement regarding the system of healing. "In Mississippi quacks grade all the way from ignorant itinerant 'hoodoo' doctors to the urbane variety who draw customers from the very elite of our population," declared Dr. R.N. Whitfield, the assistant secretary of the State Board of Health. The board went on to smudge the potential benefits of hoodoo: "Essential to the success of the 'Hoodoo' or the most pretentious quack is the ability to deceive the public into believing that he possesses a miraculous cure for any complaint." By insisting on this

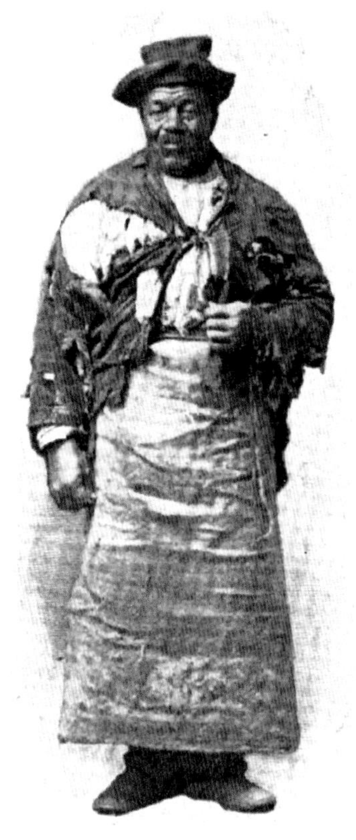

This is an early depiction of a "plantation oracle" in the late 1800s. *Courtesy of* Frank Leslie's Popular Monthly, *Volume XLIV, July to December 1897.*

logic, the State of Mississippi appeared to assure its citizens that any form of spiritual healing was dubious at best.

The fear of African healing systems would continue to affect national decisions regarding health and disease. In 1958, a number of schoolchildren in Atlanta, Georgia, became sick with an allergy that was later believed to be traced back to a specific artifact. "Voodoo" dolls from Haiti were believed to be the culprit following an importation of small dolls made from cashew nuts and jequirity beans. Newspapers alleged that a "hoodoo" was connected with the importation of the dolls. The fear of the dolls spread throughout the United States, with officials in cities such as Canton, Ohio, removing dolls from local shops. Almost twenty years later, the perceived threat of African traditions was feared to be entering the schoolhouses of rural Mississippi in April 1976 as students from a Mount Pleasant, Mississippi school started exhibiting strange behaviors. Officials noted that over fifteen students and several teachers had suddenly begun fainting at Sand Flats High School. Local papers reported, "Teachers and students who have seen the spells said the girls suddenly fall to the ground, kicking and shouting 'Don't let it get me' and 'Get it off!" The attacks last from a few minutes to as long as fifteen minutes. Some pupils contend that one girl has been putting voodoo hexes on her classmates as the result of an argument over a boy. The sheriff said some of the students may have a strong belief in black magic." Marshall County sheriff Kenneth Smith brought in a state narcotics agent, a highway patrol investigator and a number of deputies to investigate the possibility of narcotics as the prime suspect of this odd behavior. Authorities found no evidence of drug use or "Voodoo."

The fear of spiritual doctors and conjurers using coercive techniques such as hypnosis and suggestion on clients became part of the paranoia, as well.

As far back as 1928, practitioners were accused of using quackery to deceive clients. Doctor J.W. Gillespie, who touted himself as a "palmist" and "hoodoo expert," had been walking the streets of Greenwood, Mississippi, selling various alleged magical objects. The self-proclaimed "doctor" promised to bring loved ones back together and to even get rid of those who might interfere in your love life. Some items Gillespie was discovered using include rabbits' feet, mercury and other traditional materials. Gillespie was warned to leave town but returned and was arrested for extorting money by false pretense.

In the 1930s, Mississippi spiritual doctor Edgar Simmons was arrested for "false pretense" after it was discovered he was collecting money for herbal remedies and various spiritual rituals. Officials claimed Simmons had allegedly "hypnotized" several women in the city, which was believed to have led to nervous conditions and insanity.

Mid-South spiritual doctors counted on the reliability of the traditional remedies that had proven successful and the work of the spiritual to bring about good health for clients. Unfortunately, in some cases, this was not enough. In Mississippi, faith healer Lula Lee King cried as she watched the health of her ten-year-old daughter begin to deteriorate. Her little girl began to cough uncontrollably and would eventually become unresponsive. King had prayed for her daughter's healing and even took the child to a local physician. Nothing seemed to help the little girl. The mother began to wonder if the problem was more than a simple illness. The mother believed that the child could have a spiritual problem. Lula decided to take the child to visit a local spiritual healer. The healer, Tobe Fullford, prescribed the use of a traditional remedy to combat some of the child's symptoms. Fullford turned to friends Pastor Alex Ward and spiritual healer J.M. Dixon. Ward and Dixon were well known in the local African American community for providing healing treatments and medicinal supplies. Reverend Ward sold a line of herbal teas called "Grandma's Teas," some topical ointments and bottles of mineral water. Dixon was believed to have knowledge of specific rituals and herbs used in healing. Together, the men concocted a treatment involving the use of a compound consisting of cream of tartar, Epsom salts and sulfur to be placed on the child's skin to fight off skin rashes.

Police were called in after the child began to choke on what was described as "regurgitated matter" in her tiny lungs. The child had been administered a number of "potions" in order to remove a hex that her mother believed

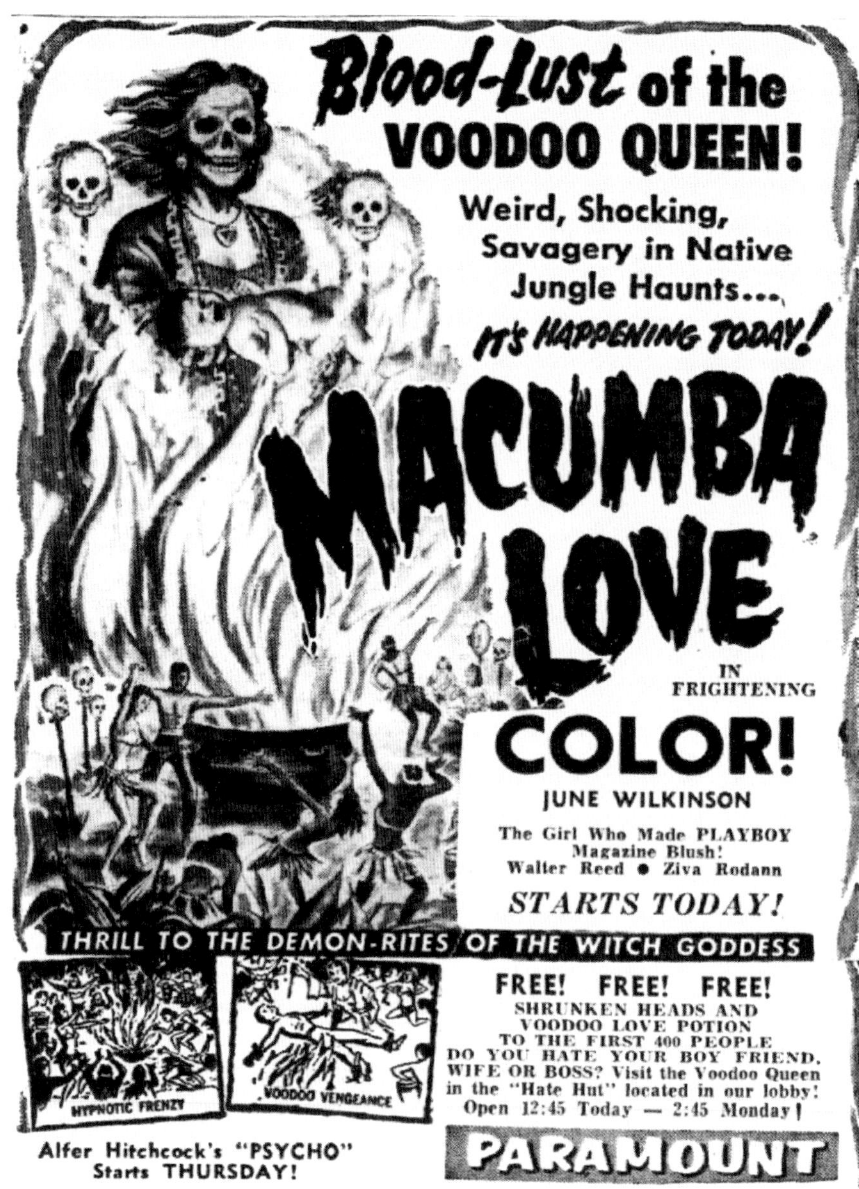

Perception of African spiritual cultures was often shaped by Hollywood. The movie *Macumba Love* played in theaters in the Mid-South offering free shrunken heads, voodoo potions and a visit to the "hate hut." *Courtesy of* Jackson Sun.

was harming the girl. The child lacked food or running water and was placed in a shack that the local district attorney described as "a shanty filled with hexes and voodoo signs." The child's mother, the spiritual healers and the minister were all charged by police for the child's death.

Conjure and the Church

Reverend William W. Colley was recognized as the only African American Baptist to have served as an appointed missionary of both a white-administered missionary agency and a black-administered missionary agency. He was appointed to serve as a missionary to Africa by the Southern Baptist Convention in 1875 and later as a missionary with an African American Baptist association known as the Baptist Foreign Missions Conference. In the fall of 1880, the membership of Beale Street Baptist invited Reverend Colley to speak to the congregation about work being performed in Africa. That continent held an important place in the hearts and minds of church members, as the church itself was built by many former slaves. The missionary spoke of ministry work being done in Africa and the pride that the black community should have for the work and people of Africa. He spoke about the evil of "witch-doctors" and "Voodoo" in Africa as he displayed several artifacts to members of the congregation. Earlier in the year, newspapers had reported that he would be speaking in the Carolinas and would be displaying "African curiosities, collected while there among which are specimens of the African gods." In Memphis, on Beale Street, the women in the congregation were noted as being particularly interested in what were called "voodoo bags" on display at the church. (One of the reasons this may have resonated with the congregants was that the use of mojo and "nation" bags or sacks were popular during this time in Memphis and on Beale.) As the missionary spoke on the threat of voodoo in Africa, he also mentioned the practice of African-derived practices in the South. A reporter noted that "Mr. Colley explained that to believe in conjuring was superstition. And he hoped no one present believed in it." The reporter noticed that "Several voices were heard saying 'Yes, sir, dey do believe in it; dey all believe in it.'" The reporter worked for a Memphis-based newspaper that reported, "This closed the entertainment and as our reporter left the building, he heard several colored men say 'He's one of dem conjurers hissel' referring to the visiting speaker."

Many churches in the Mid-South viewed rootworking and conjure-related practices as being of the devil. In October 1954, Bethel Baptist Church, an African American house of worship in Meridian, Mississippi, called local police when it was discovered that two men had placed a mysterious powder throughout the church. Powder had been poured around the pulpit, in the pastor's study and in a number of chairs. The congregation members told police that they believed the men were attempting to "hoodoo" the pastor and the church itself. In traditional hoodoo-related practices, powder was frequently used in an attempt to "cross" an enemy. The belief was that if someone came into contact with the powder or stepped over it, they would suffer.

Some ministers rallied against these traditional folk practices in sermons and publications. A 1961 tent revival in Jackson, Tennessee, featured a Reverend C.R. Graham, who was promoting his sermon series "Root Doctors, Fortune Tellers, Conjure Specialists, Window Smokers and Hair Hiders: How They Operate." Traditional African practices were viewed by many as the bane of the black community. Some churches felt that hoodoo-related practices were not only spiritually dangerous but also posed a physical threat to the community. Five years later, an evangelist traveling through the Mid-South preached against the evils of African practices. The Reverend Henry T. Beyer claimed to have been "Converted in New Orleans from a background of Hoodooism, Voodooism and Spiritualism."

The Mid-South has also been home to a number of incidents involving African folk practices such as hoodoo within churches. One of the fascinating phenomena in Memphis hoodoo history was the crossing of social networks and cultures. Ministers, rootworkers and conjurers formed relationships in this network and in some cases took the role of all three of these offices. Many academics have noted the alleged African folk practices associated with Memphis-based Church of God in Christ founder C.H. Mason and his use of roots and spiritual practices. Another personality who worked both in the pulpit and with various aspects of the rootworking culture was Bishop A.B. McEwen. Bishop McEwen had been ordained as a minster by Bishop Mason and served as a minister in Covington and Muray City, Tennessee.

As curio companies like Lucky Heart Cosmetics out of Memphis began offering cosmetics and hoodoo-related curios such as oils, powders and herbs to primarily African American customers, they also began expanding into a number of unique markets. Among these markets were churches and religious organizations. Bishop McEwen was instrumental in bringing Lucky Heart Cosmetics into church conventions. This controversial marketing of

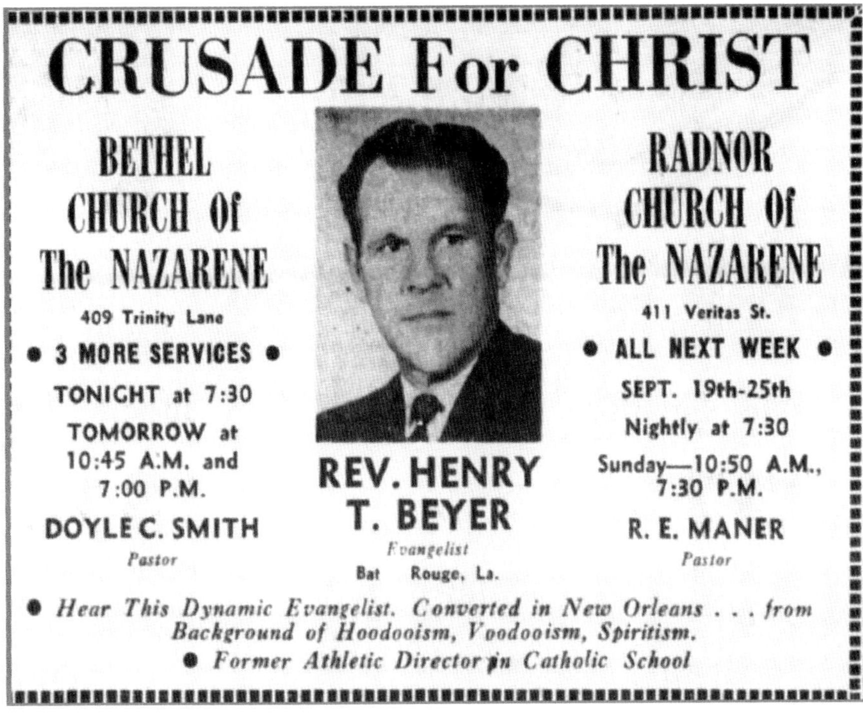

Many churches in the Mid-South rallied against rootwork and any form of African healing or spiritual practices. *Courtesy of author's collection.*

hoodoo-related products—often deemed "witchcraft" by some—into church conventions was a bold move by McEwen.

Following Bishop McEwen's death in 1969, his role in the hoodoo curio culture remained a secret to many in the church community. Personal interviews with rootworkers and curio shop owners from this period reveal that many knew of his work as both a minister and curio salesman. One shop owner shared that he knew McEwen personally and that McEwen would travel around West Tennessee speaking at churches. His presentation usually included messages about the mission work that was being in done in countries like Africa. Following the message, he would take several cosmetic items and place them on a table in front of the sanctuary. He instructed members of the congregation to leave a dime and pick up an item. The last person to leave a dime would win a prize contained in a large box that was on display with the items. The lucky person who won the box soon discovered that the box was actually a sales kit from Lucky Heart Cosmetics and that they became a salesperson

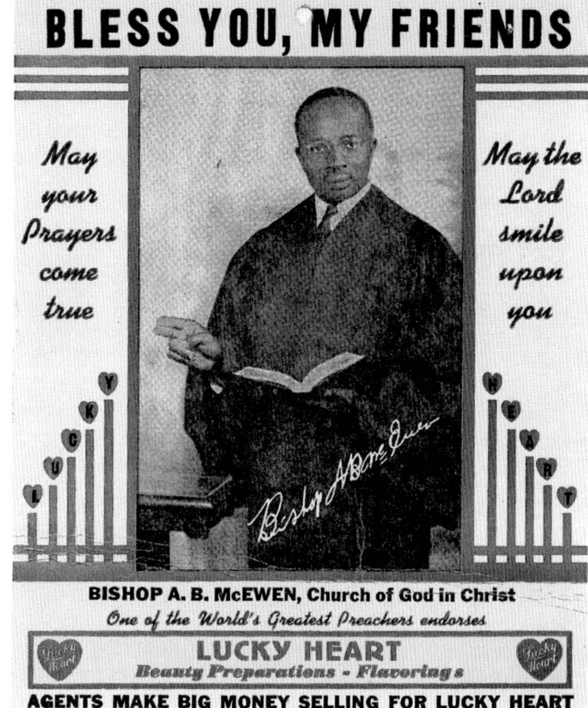

Bishop A.B. McEwen served in the Memphis-based Church of God in Christ and as a sales agent for the Lucky Heart Cosmetics Company. *Courtesy of author's collection.*

for the company. McEwen was allegedly seen driving around Memphis in a luxury car that was given to him by the owners of Lucky Heart. Bishop McEwen became the face of the church community for Lucky Heart Cosmetics, as his photo was frequently used as an endorsement of cosmetics and curios. He is credited with creating the formula for Lucky Heart Cosmetics' "Four Way" line of products.

I spoke with a minister in Humboldt, Tennessee, in 2016 who shared a story about how certain spiritual curios are still being used by some ministers in West Tennessee. One particular throat spray promised to spiritually empower ministers to be able to "whoop." Whooping is a gasping sound that marks the intake of air and is interpreted by some as the presence of the Holy Spirit during preaching. The pastor said he used the product a few times but then became convicted that he was relying on a product and not his deity for guidance during his sermons.

The mixture of spiritual workers and traditional churches could be seen in a 1949 court case in Jackson, Tennessee. The case focused on the prosecution of the spiritual leader of a Spiritualist temple for allegations of mail fraud. Bishop Willie S. Sheffield, leader of the International United

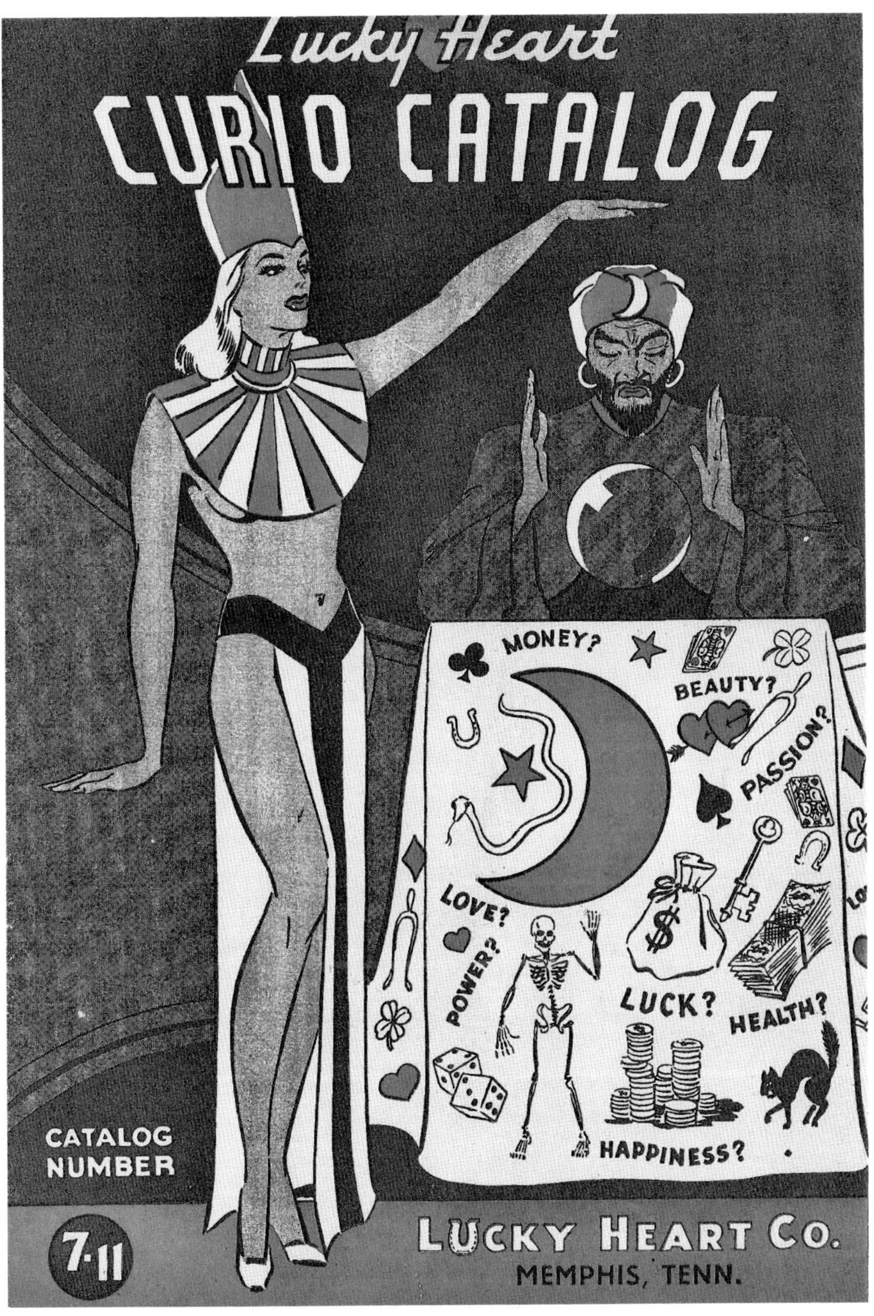

Mid-South curio companies like Lucky Heart Cosmetics employed a number of African American men and women as door-to-door sales agents. Catalogues like this were used by agents to show products that were available to customers. *Courtesy of author's collection.*

Revelation People's Spiritualist Temple of Applied Christianity in Jackson, was brought up on charges of using the postal system to con believers. Sheffield's witnesses claimed that the spiritual leader could cure sickness. He had performed prayers that could remove pain even over the phone. The leader would practice "laying on" of hands on his clients to remove their ailments. The judge observed that the healer did not do any harm, and a jury found that he actually gave sound advice to his clients. Bishop Sheffield was released with no charges. The bishop would go on to lead the People's New Way Spiritualist Church on Church Street in Jackson.

The town of Alexander City, Alabama, is home to a fascinating murder mystery involving conjure and religions that is so compelling that famed southern writer Harper Lee (author of *To Kill a Mockingbird*) wanted to write a novel based on the story. The tale of Reverend Willie Maxwell begins with the mysterious death of his wife, Mary Edwards Maxwell, who was discovered beaten and strangled in a car in 1969. The minister was indicted for murdering his wife, but before the trial could begin, the principal star witness in the case married Maxwell and then changed her testimony against him. Two years later, Maxwell's brother was found dead of excessive alcohol consumption on a rural road. An investigator with the local sheriff's department determined that the victim, Columbus Maxwell, may have been forced to drink a fatal amount of alcohol.

Two years later, the minister's second wife was found dead in a car near their home. The cause was "acute asthmatic bronchitis," which has a similar effect to suffocation. Maxwell went to court, contending that his wife died of shock after the accident and that he should receive her insurance benefits. Three years later, Maxwell's nephew was found dead in his car. The cause of death was determined to have come from him driving off the road. The victim, James Hicks, had several papers regarding insurance policies that had been taken out on his life by his mother. However, it was determined that the papers had actually been filled out in Reverend Willie Maxwell's handwriting.

It was rumored that Reverend Maxwell was a good preacher, but he was also known for "dabbling" in conjure. Maxwell was allegedly seen hanging chickens in the trees around his property. He was also seen painting his doorstep with the blood from chickens. Rumor in the African American community was that he had worked with the famous "Seven Sisters of Algiers" and had a secret room where he performed spells in his home. Interviews with people from the community reveal that many people were scared of Maxwell and would go inside their homes when he drove through the neighborhood. He established quite a reputation for preaching for the Lord and also crossing with the spirits.

On June 11, 1977, Maxwell's stepdaughter Shirley Ann Ellington was discovered dead. The police report vaguely described the death as unusual and, like many of the others related to Maxwell, took place on a rural country road. The body of the girl was discovered under a car, where it appeared that she had been changing a tire. Local opinion was that the child was dead before she was placed under the car. On June 20, Reverend Maxwell delivered the eulogy for his sixteen-year-old stepdaughter at a local funeral home. As Maxwell exchanged glares with locals who feared and suspected him of the worst, little Shirley Ann Ellington's uncle made his way through the crowd and placed a pistol against the temple of Willie Maxwell. The crowd of three hundred onlookers gasped as Robert Lewis Burns announced, "He killed Shirley and he is going to pay for it!" Burns fired three bullets into Maxwell's face.

DEDICATION

The Dedication Services for the

SPIRITUALIST SANCTUARY

WAY OF THE CROSS

LOCATED ON INSTITUTE STREET WILL BE HELD ALL DAY SUNDAY, JUNE 8, 1952.

Speakers will include various ministers of the city. Music furnished by the local quartette.

Guest speakers for the evening: Rev. A. Campbell and Madam Moore.

The Public is Invited.

A Special Invitation Is Extended to My White Friends.

REV. MARY MEARING,

Pastor.

Many Mid-South Spiritualist churches included elements of African spirituality and healing cultures within a Judeo-Christian structure. *Courtesy of* Jackson Sun.

Maxwell's legacy has burned into the memory of the community of Alexander City. Evidence of Maxwell's conjuring was discovered after his death. Family members went into the Maxwell house and discovered a number of items, including jars filled with blood. Some jars were labeled "love," "hate," "friendship" and "death." At Maxwell's funeral, Reverend C. Mardis compared Maxwell to Moses, saying he was "a murderer and a fugitive" and that "he was sent by God to lead his people." Mardis went on to say, "They accused him of being Beelzebub, they talked about him casting out the Spirit with spirits." He went on to say that Maxwell "is coming back to judge someday."

The years following the shooting of Willie Maxwell in Alexander City were filled with rumor and legend that Maxwell would return from the dead to haunt his enemies. So far, he has not returned.

HOODOO AND THE LAW

There were several undercover operations performed in the Mid-South by police that focused on targeting rootworkers and spiritual doctors. In some cases, officers would pose as clients seeking help from spiritual advisors; in other cases, officers posed as spiritual healers themselves. Montgomery, Alabama police detective Mike Chisholm became known as the department's "voodoo expert and counter-voodoo propagandist." Chisholm carried around mock curios used in hoodoo, including a bag that he made from the packaging that fruit was delivered in that contained dead spiders and flies. In one particular case, Chisholm was called to take a report on a minister who believed himself to be crossed. As many spiritual doctors would do, the detective insisted on searching the man's residence for any evidence of bewitching. Not finding anything, the detective tossed his mock mojo hand behind a piece of furniture. Retrieving it, Chisholm shined an ultraviolet light onto the bag. The flies and spiders inside began to glow eerily. The minister was told to bury the item in the backyard in order to uncross himself. As the minister began to shovel dirt on top of the hand, he immediately began to show signs of relief. A similar case involved a woman who had discovered a mysterious powder on her front step. The woman almost destroyed her front steps in an attempt to remove any negative workings that had been performed against her. The detective was called to her residence and performed a mock ritual in which he cursed the person who left the powder.

In some cases, it was believed that authorities could "detect" a practitioner of African folk traditions. Practitioners were frequently called "voo-doos." In Alabama, it was believed that you could determine if someone was a practitioner if they used healing or magical rituals. In March 1938, a vooddoo was detected, as it was observed that he had visited an elderly blind man and had promised to restore the man's sight by "throwing a spell."

Later that same year, Arkansas spiritualist Reverend H. Coheley came under investigation by postal officials in Washington, D.C. Reverend Coheley had been barred from sending out flyers offering mojo "lucky" bags for new customers. Coheley billed himself in the advertisements as the "man from Algiers" who "knows all and sees all." The minister's ads claimed that he could remove "jinxes" and could designate "lucky days."

In an odd sequence of events, police were sometimes called on the advice of spiritual workers. In August 1937, a young couple in Athens, Tennessee, visited a local spiritual reader. The reader had such a powerful reputation that some said she could "walk de wall backward." She was believed by many to have clairvoyant abilities that allowed her to see how others would die. The reader told the young couple that their niece was going to be involved in a lot of trouble that evening and that they should do whatever it took to stop her from leaving their house. The couple called the local police and had the little girl locked up in jail at the advice of the reader.

Conjurers in the Mid-South faced the constant threat of arrest by police. In 1951, a Memphis conjurer named Bell Gillum was arrested after it was discovered she was providing spiritual and medicinal treatments for locals. The sixty-nine-year-old spiritual worker had been accused of dispensing medicines without a license to members of a local army depot. Local police sent an undercover informant into the home of the woman—who was known locally as a "witchdoctor"—to observe her spiritual services. The informant complained that he had a headache and had been experiencing bizarre dreams. Bell Gillum was alleged to have boiled an iron kettle of water above a gas stove and then filled it with dried herbs, including John the Conqueror, furniture polish and rattlesnake oil. The informant claimed that the woman sat down on a three-legged stool and began to chant about the "devil's plague" until the water came to a boil. She then poured the concoction into a cup and demanded that the informant drink it. When the informant hesitated, Gillum rubbed a yellow substance into the informant's hair then rubbed a black, oily substance on the informant's head and repeated her request: "Drink it!" The informant drank the substance and began to have a burning sensation in his stomach. Gillum charged the informant ten dollars and assured him that he was now healed. Police would later arrest Gillum on charges of practicing medicine without a license. Memphis police lieutenant W.H. Ragadale reported finding bottles of rattlesnake oil, colored powders, dried herbs and "vile"-smelling oils in Gillum's home.

The history of rootwork and conjure in the Mid-South is filled with stories of racism and violence against African Americans. Folk medicine was frequently blamed for crimes, illnesses and even murders. In 1957, jailers for the Hinds County Jail in Greenville, Mississippi, blamed "Voodoo medicine" for injuries that prisoners received while in their care. The victims were placed in a "hot box" or solitary confinement cell and then beaten with a leather strap. The men who were arrested were part of a group of men who were searching for money using a "voodoo machine" that appeared similar to a compass. The sheriff's department described the men as going through "black magic rites." The four men had rubbed "voodoo" medicine over their bodies to keep police away as they searched for money.

It was not uncommon for police to discover hoodoo-related evidence in areas of the Mid-South. Birmingham, Alabama police discovered the victim of a shooting on the south side of the city. A local coroner was called to examine the body. The victim, John Deason, was discovered with a collection of traditional conjure items. The following is a list of what police discovered among the victim's personal belongings.

A hoodoo bag containing a dead frog and a rabbit's foot both old and dry.
A brass coin of uncertain origin.
A rusty horseshoe nail.
A piece of quartz.
A conjure bag, consisting of small roots sewed up in some kind of skin.
A brass check.
A sack of tobacco.
A piece of red flannel soaked in some kind of oil, probably skunk oil.
A number of variously shaped buttons and $1.84 in money.

Murders

Fear of the power of conjure has historically made many southerners do some extreme things. Among the more extreme, tragically, have been incidents in which spiritual workers are targeted and murdered. As far back as 1901, there have been recorded incidents in which rootworkers have been murdered. In 1901, in Vicksburg, Mississippi, a spiritual doctor was killed by a man who he believed had cursed him. Fred Gay confessed to killing Solomon Russell to stop the effects of a spiritual working that Russell was believed to have sent. Following the murder, Gay performed a protection ritual that included the creation of a circle around his residence. The circle included materials such as blue stone, salt and red pepper. Gay told authorities that this was done to keep away any spirits that Russell would have sent after him.

In 1914, Joe Cook, a rootworker in Jonestown, a town in Coahoma County, Mississippi, was murdered by George Reynolds. Reynolds was being sentenced to death for the murder of Cook when he began to tell the judge about the circumstances surrounding the case. Reynolds's wife had become very ill and was acting very strangely. Her husband believed that she had been "conjured" and that Cook was the responsible party.

Reynolds told the judge that he believed the only way he could break the horrible curse was to kill the conjurer himself. The judge, seeing the husband's dilemma and obvious respect for the power of conjure, instead sentenced Reynolds to life in prison.

In April 1928, in Holly Springs, Mississippi, farmhand Mack Bowen was living on a plantation owned by Mrs. Elbert Jones. Bowen had become sick and feared for his life. He believed that he had been crossed and traveled into the city to find some form of protection. Bowen visited local druggist Howard Jones for help after he produced evidence of his bewitching in the form of pieces of old quilts, bird nests, marbles and a broken cane. Bowen insisted that these items were proof that he would soon be walking on crutches should this conjure work on him. The druggist gave Bowen some medicines as well as some charms to protect himself from the working. Bowen returned home to find a man admiring his wife whom he had previously warned not to return to his property. The local papers describe Bowen as "driven wild by the hoodoo" when he shot the admirer and the man's horse. Bowen then proceeded to track down the alleged conjurer who had crossed him, a spiritual doctor who went by the name of Charlie Balfour. Balfour was ninety years old. Bowen, in desperation, killed the doctor in order to try to break the spell.

Several years later, in 1943, Memphis native Chester Williams shot his wife and threw her body over a bridge of the Hatchie River, claiming that she used "voodoo" to harm him. He told Memphis police that "voodoo ruined my life." Six years later, Alberta Jefferson, a Knoxville woman knocked twenty-six-year-old Obie Roberts down a flight of stairs and then shot him. Jefferson told police that Roberts was a "voodoo doctor" and had placed a "death hex" on her that had made her blood pressure rise and her neck stiffen and had negatively affected her heart. Killing the spiritual doctor was believed to have released her from this curse. In 1950, a similar case in Greenville, Mississippi, developed in which a man shot and killed a suspected conjurer because it was believed that he had placed a crossing (a term used to denote being cursed) on the victim.

A high-profile case involving the murder of a spiritual worker occurred in 1957 in Shelbyville, Tennessee. The victim was killed because his client believed he had placed a curse on him. Forty-year-old Mose M. Martin from Stevenson, Alabama, had sought guidance from spiritual worker Simon T. Warner, known for his healing and psychic abilities in the Mid-South.

Mose drove up from Alabama to seek help for digestive problems he was having with his stomach. Warner charged him sixty dollars for a spiritual treatment that was intended to remove Mose's ailment. After leaving the healer's home, Mose began to feel severe discomfort and fear. He began to perspire as his heart raced. His head filled with fears of dabbling with magic and thoughts of worry.

Mose could feel a spiritual rope tightening across his chest. It became difficult to breathe. He would lie awake at night, staring at the ceiling, sometimes clutching the tattered cover of an old Holy Bible next to his side. Mose worried that it was no longer the stomachache that haunted him but the insidious spirits that the "spirit doctor" had loosened on him. He could not take any more of the psychological torture from the white spiritualist who had performed this mysterious operation on him. Mose reached into the bureau beside his bed and retrieved a .32 caliber pistol.

The eighty-five-mile trek from Stevenson to Shelbyville, Tennessee, seemed to take forever. Mose's car sputtered and spurred as a cold rain began to fall across the highway. Mose could almost feel the relief that he was about to experience when he would break the spell that haunted him. On arriving at Simon Warner's place, Mose slipped his pistol into the back of his pants.

Warner met him at the door with a smile and a greeting. "Nice to see you again Mister Mose, what can I do for you today?" Mose's heart began to race again as he mumbled, "There's something I need to talk to you about. Something important." Warner closed the door behind him and began to walk down a long hall on creaking wooden floors. Mose's breathing became louder as his eyes scanned the walls of the home. Paintings of planetary symbols and strange-looking mythical animals adorned the hall. As the two entered a room, Warner turned around and smiled at Mose. "Hope you're feeling better. Last time we met you weren't doing so well."

As Warner closed the door to the consultation room, Mose Martin stared at the crystal ball and tarot cards spread across a wood table. For a moment, he worried that Warner might come back to haunt him from the grave. But none of that mattered now. This crossing, this curse that Warner had placed on him was killing him physically and spiritually. Mose reached back into the bottom of his shirt and presented the pistol to Warner's chest. "What? What are you doing?," Warner cried out. Mose's eyes bulged with intensity as he felt the nose of the pistol finding resistance against Simon Warner's chest. "I'm about to set myself free, conjure man. I ain't no fool, I know you put a curse on me and I'm about to break it free!" Mose Martin fired five shots from the pistol into Simon Warner.

Following the discovery of the body, local police put out an all-points bulletin to all regional law enforcement agencies. Mose Martin was stopped more than an hour away from the scene of the murder. Martin and his girlfriend, Pearl Hutchinson, were stopped by the Alabama Highway Patrol. Martin confessed to the crime. It was documented that Martin testified to police, "I shot him because he double-crossed me in voodoo. He admitted before I shot him that he double-crossed me. I would have shot anybody who double-crossed me in black magic like he did." Warner would go on to testify in the Davidson County Jail that he believed that the shooting did not break the curse. Instead, he claimed that a magical string was being tightened across his body. He told a local reporter for the *Tennessean*, "The string is still around me," as he removed his shirt to reveal that there was nothing visible around his stomach. Martin testified that Simon Warner told him that he would never get well. He continued, "I waited for it to go. I don't think it'll ever go now. There's no other way to break it. If you were killing me wouldn't that be enough reason for me to kill you?"

Simon Warner's legacy as a spiritual worker while he was alive was prolific. Warner discovered that he had spiritual powers at the age of ten. He soon became well known for being able to predict various incidents. When his powers of perception became known in the community, many people

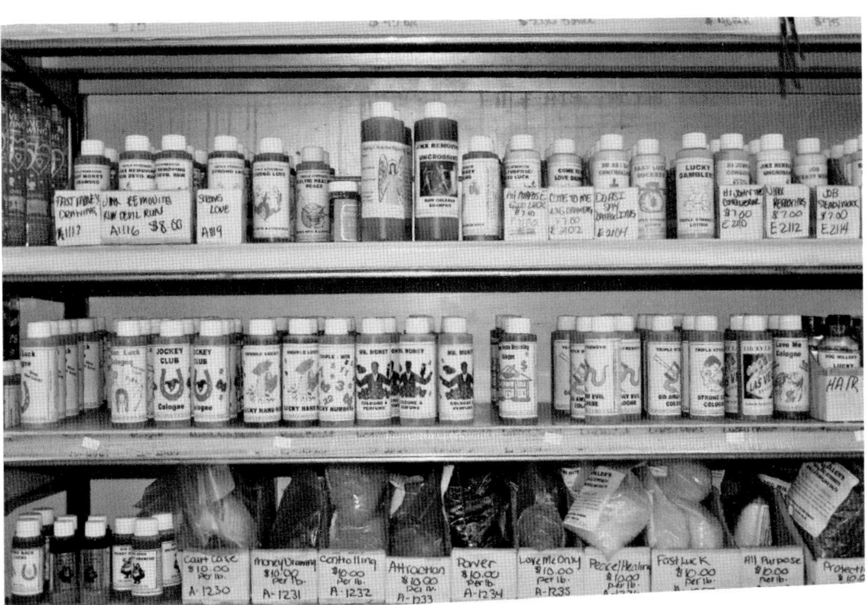

There have historically been a number of spiritual supply shops in the Mid-South that carry materials used in rootworking and conjure. *Courtesy of author's collection.*

began to seek his assistance in finding lost materials, lost loves and financial guidance. Warner recalled one experience in which two men approached him about getting his guidance in locating a buried treasure. A group of Native Americans was said to have buried a chest of gold, and the men promised to give Warner two dollars if he could locate the gold. Warner told the men, "Thank you" and said that if he could locate it, he would keep it and give them the two dollars.

Warner became famous in 1941, when he supernaturally located the body of a missing Chapel Hill woman. When police found the body, news about Warner spread throughout the world. He began to receive hundreds of letters every day asking for his assistance in locating objects and people as well as questions about love. Warner became known as the "Crime Doctor," using what he called "character readings" to see into the supernatural. He developed an ability to see when someone was going to die. He would frequently work with law enforcement to provide them with insight into when he would foresee a potential murder in the community. In 1945, the "Shelbyville Seer," as he became known locally, helped in bringing a fugitive to justice when an African American farmer had beat his seven-year-old niece with a piece of wood. Police searched for two days to locate Andrew Fagan. He turned up at Simon Warner's residence seeking advice. Warner consulted the spirits and advised Fagan to turn himself in. The seer accompanied Fagan to the local police department, where he surrendered to local authorities.

Warner went on to study criminology and created a "crime show" exhibit that he wanted to take around the world. The $75,000 collection featured a number of mannequins dressed as famous criminals, including Adolf Hitler and John Dillinger, and was focused on curbing juvenile crime. Warner had a half sister known locally as "Granny Jones" who was practiced in folk healing. She was also known as an effective spiritual reader who used playing cards to divine the future. Residents tell of taking their children to see her for healing. Granny (aka "Bessie Jones") was known to have the power to remove warts, burns and scars through various rituals.

Some rootworkers and conjurers have been killed because of what their assailants viewed as a lack of effectiveness. In Vicksburg, Mississippi, a spiritual worker was murdered by one of his clients after the working he had performed failed. The Reverend Henry B. Johnson promised to "hoodoo" the dice of his client, fifty-year-old ex-convict C.C. Moore. He was so confident in his spiritual services that he promised a "money back

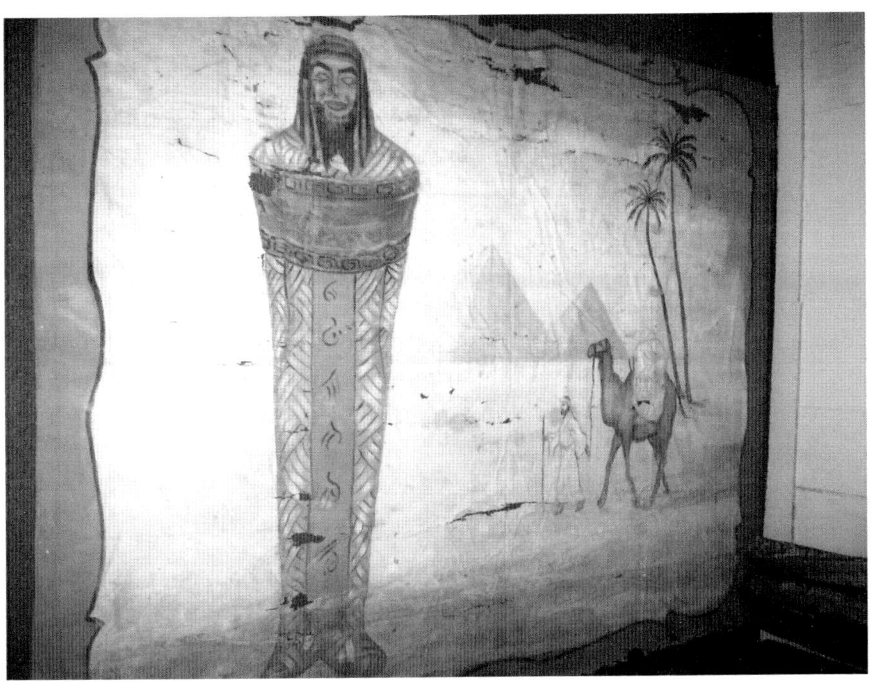

A part of spiritual worker Simon Warner's traveling museum. Warner became known as the "Seer of Shelbyville." *Courtesy of eBay.*

guarantee." The client continued to lose and later confronted the minister. Johnson refused to pay, and Moore attacked him, beating him about the head and cutting his throat.

As African-derived religions and healing practices were constantly blamed for crime, murder and deviancy in the Mid-South, some chose to blame acts of terrorism on devotees of these practices. In March 1956, a Brookhaven, Mississippi man was investigated by police after a bomb exploded in a post office in New Orleans, Louisiana. Three days before the bomb exploded, a letter was sent to a local police department threatening to blow it up. The letter read:

> *We are so high you cannot climb over us, so low you cannot get beneath us and so broad you cannot get around us so you must go through us or by us. You must go straight. Your name has been handed us as a rat and a double crosser. To this we give you 10 days warning to get back in line or go where you just left or else stand the consequences. You may run but you can't hide. We will make you melt away like dry ice in a vapor on a hot day and lose*

> *everything. No one will be able to help you.* ["Lincoln Man Bomb Suspect," Clarion-Ledger, March 14, 1956]

The threat appeared to specifically target one or a number of individuals. As puzzling as it was, the signature was even more puzzling. The letter was signed "Marie LeVeau III, Queen of the Voodoo."

CONJURE IN THE COURTROOM

Courtrooms in the Mid-South had come to witness a number of cases involving rootwork and conjure throughout the years. In 1899, a judge heard a case involving two conjurers who sold a defective charm to a client. The conjurers had charged seven dollars for a charm that was alleged to secure employment, good health and an abundance of work. One of the men gave the client what was described as a "hoodoo jack or hand." The charm consisted of a small piece of lodestone wrapped in a red flannel cloth. Apparently, after carrying the charm for a period of time, the client decided that it was ineffective. He approached the two conjurers and asked for his money back. After receiving only a portion of the money back, the client, Tom Parker, took the case to the local police. The men were arrested and charged with obtaining money under false pretenses.

In October 1925, a courtroom in Jackson, Mississippi, listened to a curious tale from witnesses who spoke against spiritual worker Sarah Boyd. Boyd had been brought up on charges of disturbing the peace. While Boyd claimed to be a benevolent spiritual worker seeking to free people from their ailments, many in the courtroom saw her as a wicked conjurer. "She pulled woodchucks out of my ear," one witness testified. "She made me spit up frogs," claimed another. The courtroom of Judge J.H. Penix watched in shock as witness after witness came to the stand. One witness claimed that Sarah would get up in the middle of the night and bang on the side of her house, screaming, "I am conjuring you. I am a hoodoo!" Many of Sarah's neighbors claimed that she sold conjure bags to people in the community; as a result, the neighbors demanded she be removed from the community. "She is a hoodoo and a conjurer and we can't live in the same neighborhood with her," exclaimed witnesses. The alleged conjurer claimed that the only spiritual healing work she had done was to formulate herbal teas that were used to heal her clients. Boyd proceeded to explain to the judge what kind of ailments the teas would allegedly cure. After much insistence from her neighbors, Boyd was fined by the judge and ordered to move from the neighborhood. She explained to the judge that she had no money to pay the fine. Witnesses told the local press that Boyd then walked over to her attorney and rubbed a conjure bag against him, causing him to pay her fines to the court.

In Prentiss, Mississippi, home to blues legend Tommy Johnson, authorities scoffed at the use of conjure-related practices. In 1933, a local believer in conjure sprinkled powder in the chairs of courtroom attorneys during the court's lunch break. An attorney assisting the prosecuting district attorney was given an "extra dose" of the powder, according to witnesses. Local newspapers concluded, "Whether Mr. Hall [Prentiss, Mississippi district attorney Toxey Hall] and his associates are impervious to 'hoodoo dust' or whether the dust lost its magical qualities by some hook or crook, is not known." The reporter covering this incident also advised, "It would be well for other district attorneys over Mississippi to look into the matter and see if they are 'hoodoo dust' resistant."

2
TRADITIONAL REMEDIES AND RITUALS

Blues avenue is plumb "root conscious."
—Nat D. Williams

Legendary Memphian and civil rights champion Nat D. Williams, who was born on Beale Street, was very vocal about the power of roots and her respect toward traditional African American practices using herbs in the Mid-South.

> *Beale Street is a buzz about roots. Yeah plain old back and graveyard roots. Blues avenue is plumb "root conscious." As a matter of fact the "street of a thousand shades" has been "root-ish" all along. But this "corner" can't recall when this subject has been brought out in open air conversation before. Anyway the other day a group of the boys got to focusing various and sundry angles on the root topic. And friends brought on more talk, talk that veered over into the spirit world and then engaged back onto the grimy pavements of Beale Street when the blues began. The confab started when one of the fellows expressing doubt as to the efficacy of some herb medicine he'd been imbibing for quite a spell in an effort to combat a certain rheumatic twing that was camping around his left hip. It seems that his favorite root doctor had started off his treatments with a whitish looking concoction. And three or four bottles of that white medicine seemed to be doing him all the good in the world. He was about to be on the road to huckle bucking. And here the doctor had changed the color of the medicine to a chocolate brown…his color! Who in the world ever heard of a dark root juice doing a dark man any good?*

Yes sir that Beale Streeter was plumb disgusted. But another brother was equally disgusted at his remarks. In fact a couple of the brethren registered various shades of aversion to his assertions. One guys angle was "It's a dad-gummed shame that we got folks still living who believe in witch doctors, yes sir thats all it is just plain voodoo or conjure mess."

Traditional Remedies

Mid-South rootworkers had a wide variety of remedies utilizing plants, animals and various household materials. The following is a collection of some of the remedies recorded throughout the Mid-South.

Asthma: To combat asthma, a healer would first measure the client. The healer would then cut a tree branch down and cut it to match the height of the client. The stick would be kept in a corner of the room alongside the sick client. Another technique would be to place a rabbit's tail inside the client's pillow. The client would be instructed to sleep on the pillow to cure the asthma. Some remedies became controversial to outsiders of the culture. In 1959, Memphis spiritual doctor Eugene Carey was arrested by police as he was caught rubbing down a female client with kerosene to cure her of asthma.

Bleeding: Some healers used coal oil to stop bleeding.

Boils: Healers used a number of ingredients, including cow manure and crushed jimson weed, to remove boils.

Burns: One remedy for burns used crushed corn husks and sulfur to make a compound to rub on the burn.

Carbuncle: The infected abscess would be treated with a mixture of poke root and water. They were boiled and combined with chips of sarsaparilla, bodock (also known as "Osage Orange") and rue (also known as "Daylilies").

Colds: The common cold had a number of diverse treatments. One technique involved using yellowroot or quinine. Some healers would have clients sip turpentine and sugar to fight off colds and bad coughs. The traditional cord of asafetida was also placed around the neck of clients to fight off the cold. One remedy in West Tennessee included pouring castor oil on the head to get rid of the cold.

Constipation: Some healers would boil apple roots and poke salat into a tea to help clients with constipation. One West Tennessee healer shared that she used snuff, turpentine and various herbs to create a paste that the client would place in the rectum in order to heal constipation.

Croup: One technique used by healers in the Mid-South involved hanging a copper penny around the neck of their client in order to get rid of the croup.

Earaches: Healers would frequently blow smoke into the ear of their clients to bring relief to earache pain. Some would spit the juice from tobacco into the ear. Sweet oil was also applied in some cases to relieve the earache.

Measles: An East Tennessee–based healer was known to use a tea made from sheep droppings to treat measles. A Mississippi-based remedy was to administer catnip or sage tea.

Mumps: A Mississippi-based cultural informant advised that she would use hog jowl to cure the mumps. The jowl was boiled; the jelly that was produced would be rubbed on the body of the client.

Nose bleeds: Hog lard was rubbed inside the nostril while reading a Bible verse.

Piles: The term *piles* is a folk word used to describe hemorrhoids. Folklorists in Mississippi have documented families speaking of treatments utilizing a technique in which a cork stopper is burnt. The ashes from the cork are mixed with Vaseline. The client is advised to dip their pointing finger into the substance and apply it to their rectum. I documented a similar technique used by a West Tennessee rootworker that utilized poke root, snuff and turpentine to create a similar concoction applied in the same manner.

Poison oak: A mixture of gunpowder and lead was rubbed into the infected area of the skin.

Rashes: One treatment used by Mid-South healers involved using a powder made from a dirt dauber nest applied to the area of the rash.

Rheumatism: A belt filled with John the Conqueror root was said to fight off rheumatism.

Skin problems: White potatoes were cut and placed in a warm bath for soaking to remedy skin problems.

Swelling: The herb mullein was boiled, and the water was used to rub around swollen regions of the body.

Teething: A popular technique found in Mississippi and Tennessee particularly involved tying the foot of a mole to a string and placing it around the infant's neck. The use of a mole's foot can be found in a number of healing traditions around the world. In England, the feet were used as amulets to remove cramps. Mole feet found in Norfolk, Virginia, were used as charms against toothaches, while in North Carolina, the feet

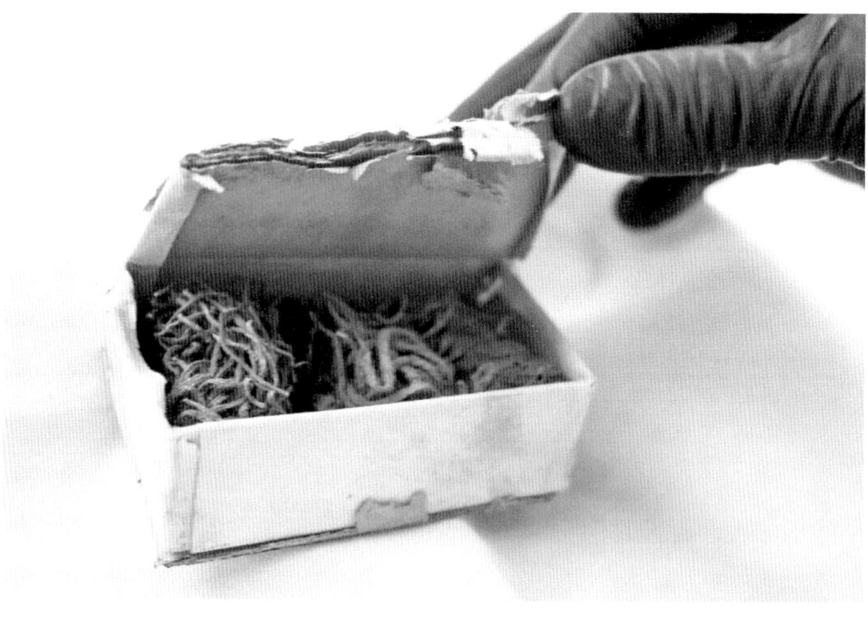

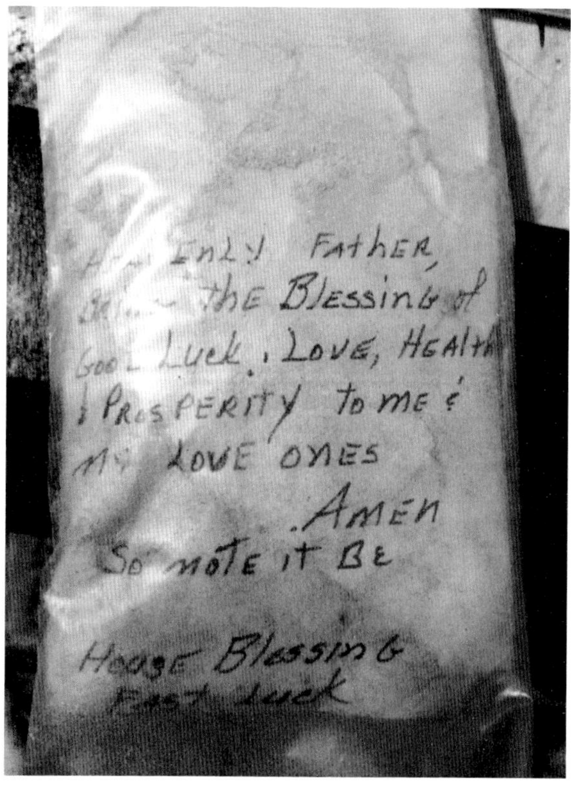

Above: The Memphis Pink Palace Museum has preserved a number of dried herbs once used by Mid-South rootworkers on Beale Street. *Courtesy of author's collection.*

Left: "Fast Luck" Powder was used to bring good luck and good health. Note the accompanying prayer used to activate the powder. *Courtesy of author's collection.*

were used to bring good luck. In the Delta, some believed that you could place an alligator tooth on a string and place it around the child's neck. When the child was tempted to bite down on something, they would bite on the alligator tooth for relief. One Mississippi-based technique was to take an egg and name it after the child that is teething. The egg would then be wrapped in cloth and hung over a doorway. When the teething has completed, the egg will have dried up.

Thrash: Hoodoo-related lore made its way into one of the healing techniques found in the Mid-South. The supernatural power residing in the seventh son or daughter in a family has been an age-old belief in southern healing cultures. Some healers believed that the seventh daughter of the seventh daughter should blow into the mouth of a client with thrash in order to bring about healing.

Worms: Some Mississippi healers would make a ring of turpentine around the client's neck and around the navel. This was believed to send the worms back down into the body.

Wounds: Some Mid-South healers would boil a hog's hoof and remove the gelatin from the hoof and apply it to the wound.

Traditional Rituals

In 1970, West Tennessee folklorist Anna Lett recorded some fascinating insights into local beliefs regarding spirits and spiritual practices in the Mid-South. Her cultural informant was a spiritual worker in Jackson, Tennessee, known as "Mama Mollie." Mama Mollie was known locally for performing spiritual readings and healings for clients. The folklorist describes how Mollie spent hours telling her about conjuring, casting spells, warding off spirits and other magical practices. She advised the folklorist that in West Tennessee male conjurers primarily taught females their craft; female conjurers were to teach male students their craft. Mama Mollie advised that in her experience, she believed that conjure would not affect a white person. Mollie shared many stories, including one about a family of conjurers that became victims of theft. The thief broke into the family's chicken coop and was discovered in the act. The family placed a spell on the thief that made him lift his hands into the air and stay standing in the same position all through the night.

Mama Mollie shared a number of practices and beliefs used by Mid-South conjurers, including the following:

- A conjurer can harm someone by taking coils of their victim's hair and scattering them around the spring where the victim gets their water.
- A conjurer can take a victim's hair and tie it to a string placed around a spring. The spring then becomes conjured, and anyone who drinks from the spring will become conjured.
- Conjurers can magically pollute streams where women wash their clothes by placing roots into the stream itself.
- Conjurers can help a person reform bad habits by sprinkling salt and sulfur over their tables and beds.
- Conjurers can sow salt in a person's yard, followed by rhymed incantations, to create an effective death charm.
- Placing a conjure bag in the path of someone who will walk over it can bring that person under the control of the conjurer.

Madam Mollie also provided information about specific materials used to conjure in the Mid-South. Some of these include:

- Those seeking to perform spellwork without the aid of a conjurer can place horsehair and needles on a doorstep to affect their victim.
- The nails and hairs of a person can be used to magically punish that person through rituals.
- To conjure another person, one can take the hair, fingernails and toenails of a victim. They then blow nine breaths into the materials and throw them away in an area where they would never pass through again. The first person to walk through that area will be conjured by the spell.
- To conjure someone, make a little wax figure, placing some of the target's hair, fingernails and any possessions belonging to them in the figure and burn it. This is used as an effective death charm.
- To conjure someone, get a bit of their blood on a cloth and place the cloth behind a rock in a chimney. Once the cloth rots, the target of the spell will die.
- To conjure someone, obtain a photograph of your target.
- A very effective love spell is to take seven hairs from a blood snake, seven scales from a rattlesnake, seven bits of feathers from an owl and a hair and nails from your target. Place them

in a fire and cook them for seven minutes in rainwater obtained during the first rain in April. Sprinkle these materials on the clothing of the target.
- Graveyard dirt can be used to conjure a well.
- One conjurer was able to use a stick and three grains of coffee to place a spell on someone.
- Bones obtained from a dead person can protect from conjure.

Madam Mollie advised that there were a number of indicators that a person might be conjured, as well as practices that can remove conjure, including the following:

- If a snake is found in a bed, it is a sign of conjure.
- Digging under the steps of someone who has conjured you will remove the spell.
- To catch a conjure, you can place something under the conjurer's doorstep, and it will trap the spell.
- To prevent conjuring, tie a piece of silver with a hole in it around your right leg.
- To prevent conjuring, wear a dime in your shoe.
- A horseshoe nailed to a door will keep off conjuring influences.
- A rabbit's foot worn around the neck will keep off spells.
- Carry red pepper in your pocket to protect yourself from conjure.
- To remove spells from drinking water, take the water across a stream.
- If you become conjured, take nine needles and put them in a dipper of water. Boil the water until the water evaporates. This will remove the conjure.
- To take off a spell, read the Bible and do something in the name of Christ.
- Salt on the front porch can protect you from spells.

In many Mid-South communities, "witches" were feared as malevolent spirits. Madam Mollie shared a number of beliefs, practices and warnings regarding witches, including the following:

- In order to become a witch, one must go to the devil at the top of the highest hill at sunrise nine successive days and curse

God. The devil then places one hand on the candidate's head and one on his feet and receives the promise that all between his hands shall be devoted to his services.

- If you put one hand on your head and one on the bottom of your feet and swear by good and evil that you will forsake all that is good and uphold the devil in all his works, you will become a wizard.
- If a woman only has one tooth in her head, she is a witch.
- A woman who has long, straight hair that curls at the ends like a drake's tail can practice magic.
- If you want to keep away witches, lay a straw broom in the doorway.
- If you are troubled by witches, place a meal sifter over your face as you sleep. When witches arrive, they must pass back and forth through every hole in the mesh. By this time, you will have sufficient sleep and can be awake.
- Throw salt into your fire to keep witches from coming down the chimney.
- The smell of frankincense, sulfur and blessed water keeps witches away.
- Boil sweet milk on the stove and stir slowly to keep away witches.

Folklorist Bill Ferris performed extensive fieldwork in Vicksburg, where he encountered rootworking culture among his cultural informants. Some of the beliefs and observations that Bill documented include the following:

- Putting red pepper and salt in your shoes will keep hexes away.
- Some people wear silver dimes to keep off spirits.
- Laying tricks can be achieved by placing objects under the front porch to step over or in the house.
- The naming of conjurers as "two-headed doctors" and "faith doctors."
- If you bury clothes in a cemetery, as they start to fade, the victim fades away.
- A frog can be placed in a pillowcase. When it begins to fade away, the victim begins to fade away.

Some additional beliefs and practices found in Mississippi and Tennessee include the following:

GENUINE
NEW ORLEANS
VAN VAN
OIL

PRICE 35c

LUCKY HEART CO.
MEMPHIS, TENN.

Left: Legendary anthropologist Zora Neale Hurston claimed that Van Van oil was the most powerful conjuring oil in Louisiana. Some Mid-South curio companies like Lucky Heart Cosmetics manufactured bottles of the oil for local spiritual supply shops. *Courtesy of author's collection.*

Below: West Tennessee spiritual worker Mother Jones (pseudonym) holds a bottle of Hoyt's Cologne. Hoyt's has been used by spiritual workers in the Mid-South for years, as it is believed to draw in good luck. *Courtesy of author's collection.*

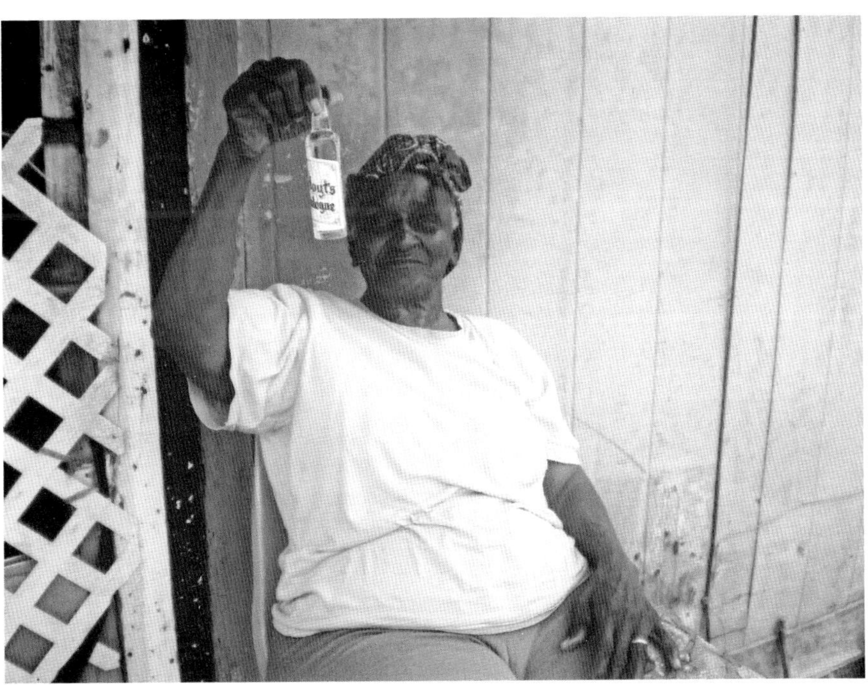

- No sweeping your broom after dark.
- Avoid burning sassafras wood.
- Be careful buying dogs. A dog that belonged to someone who died as a "sinner" will not only tree animals but will also "tree" spirits.
- Do not let hair touch the ground, as it will be picked up by a bird and placed into a bird's nest to create trouble.

TO TRACK DOWN A MURDERER

Arkansas folklorist John Quincy Wolf shared a story about a magical practice in the Delta used to track down a murderer. After the murder of an African American man, the killer escaped, running to another city. The body of the victim was discovered in a funeral home with an egg in each one of his hands. The funeral director was recorded as saying that the family of the victim had placed an egg in each hand. The family believed that when one of the eggs exploded or rotted, the murderer would return to town and could be arrested.

This same technique was documented in the 1930s in Selma, Alabama, when a young African American girl was murdered by a drunken man at a local dance. The girl's body was dressed in white clothing, and her mouth was held open by pins. This was believed to allow her to speak if her spirit wanted to call her murderer back. The mirrors in the house were covered, as it is custom to keep the spirit of the deceased from seeing themselves. An egg was then placed in each hand of the deceased. The young girl was buried after three days. Several objects were placed around her grave. Personal objects such as a fan that she carried and toys from her childhood were placed around the grave site. The razor that had been used to kill her was placed at the grave site as well. After twenty-one days, the funeral was held.

As the preacher was speaking to the loved ones of the dearly departed, he took the opportunity to denounce the murderer—and dancing, as well. As members of the family began to weep, a man made his way through the crowd to what was known as the "mourners bench." The man's clothes were torn, his skin dirty and his stare that of a wildman. He turned to the family and spoke: "Last night in the swamp she come to me....I was starved and dying. But I knew her. I've come back, I killed her but I loved her. I thought I could bring her back to life again. Now I can't...."

To Evade Uncle Sam

The U.S. government has not always looked fondly on hoodoo. In 1943, rumor around Clarke County, Mississippi, was that if you were called to enlist in the U.S. military, you could pay a visit to a particular root man in town who could help you avoid being drafted. Clarence Ainsworth had been working with roots for years and had become proficient with specific roots and energies that could give clients supernatural favor in their endeavors. Ainsworth would use a traditional John the Conqueror oil and a mass-marketed oil known as "Hindoo Magic Oil." The Hindoo Magic product was to be dropped into the client's shoes every day, and the John the Conqueror oil was poured onto a root that was to be carried in the pocket. The oil was also to be rubbed behind the ears just before any military physical examinations.

Traditional Artifacts

A number of charms have been used throughout the history of rootwork and conjure cultures of the Mid-South. Materials ranging from dried roots to animal bones were often used as charms.

The rootworking community's response to the threat of epidemic sickness in the Mid-South frequently involved the use of charms and remedies to combat risks to health and to protect communities. It is interesting to note that some communities that typically would not embrace rootworking practices actually began to use traditional remedies once scoffed at. As Memphis combatted several rounds of the yellow fever epidemic in the 1800s, many whites outside the rootwork culture who were accustomed to publicly chastising African healing cultures actually began using many of these traditional remedies. Likewise, many Mid-South charms became popular during a meningitis scare in Hope, Arkansas, in 1935. Locals began sharing information about various charms that would provide protection, including a rabbit's foot from the left side of the body, a bag of asafetida, a lamp wick for chewing and the blood of a black chicken. Seven items were to be carried, including a buckeye, an Irish potato, nutmeg, a good luck penny, a mothball, a camphor bag on the stomach and a dime around the ankle.

The charms and healing techniques used by rootworkers in the Delta were often looked on with interest by those outside of the culture. Quitman,

Mississippi, in the 1960s, became home to many practitioners of African American healing cultures. Local public-health nurse Mary Harwell began to notice a number of healing practices and charms used by many of her patients in the area. Harwell began to collect a number of charms and displayed them in the Clarke County Public Health Office. Harwell explained to a reporter: "That's my collection of protection charms taken from the necks of colored babies. I guess you might call them voodoo charms." She continued: "We don't get as many as we used to but occasionally a young mother will bring a child in decorated with a charm necklace of dogwood bark or horse nettles which they usually call 'tred ways'. [This may be a local term used to describe the horse nettles that carry the folk name "tread softlies."] The young mother usually explains that she uses the charms to appease an old granny, or an aunt who has strong beliefs in the power of such charms against illness." Harwell was said to have kept a pair of dried mole's feet on display. She explained that the feet were worn around the neck of a baby that was teething. She explained that "the old colored mammys believed that dried moles feet made teething easier for the baby." Harwell shared a mixed belief in the power of roots and spiritual healing. She claimed: "Of course this primitive folk medicine does have some basis in medical practice. After all many of our drugs are derived from plants and roots, but the belief in these charms is mostly superstition."

As many historians and folklorists alike have documented the use of coins as charms in the Delta, Nurse Harwell collected a number of coin charms that included pennies that had been drilled and placed onto a necklace as

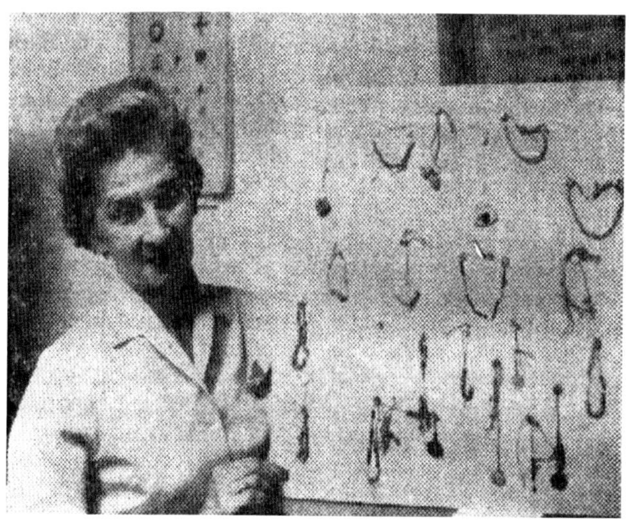

Healthcare professionals in the Mid-South have encountered a number of rootwork- and conjure-related practices and artifacts among patients. In the 1960s, Mississippi nurse Mary Harwell began collecting charms used by her patients. *Courtesy of* Clark County Tribune.

well as the Roosevelt dime being used as a charm worn by practitioners. She noted that she had seen a rise in the use of "Kennedy" coins being used as charms. Nurse Harwell noted that many families would use a tea made from the bark of dogwood leaves in order to help infants fall asleep. Little did Harwell realize the cultural and historical significance of her root and artifact display in the tiny clinic in Quitman.

One 1893 preparation used in the Delta to bring peace to a quarrelsome family combined charcoal and horsehair to make a small charm.

The Mojo Bag in the Mid-South

The use of the traditional mojo bag in African American hoodoo culture was certainly prevalent in the Mid-South. As early as 1871, there were reports of rootworkers like "Aunt Annie," an African American spiritual worker who created and sold bags on the streets of Memphis. Annie's bags sold for five dollars and were said to contain a number of materials that gave the bags their power. Early records show that among the materials contained in these bags was an animal's foot, such as from a rabbit or raccoon. Bags also included lodestone, a needle, dried herbs and a bird's beak, such as from an owl. Some bags contained animal bones and even insects.

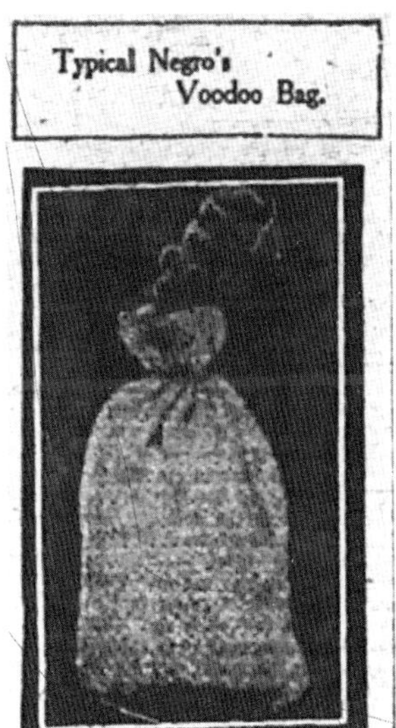

Mojo hands were frequently referred to as "voodoo bags" by those outside of the rootwork and conjure communities in the Mid-South. This is an image of a bag from Arkansas from the early 1900s. *Courtesy of* Daily Arkansas Gazette.

The power behind such bags was sometimes called into question by outsiders and unsatisfied clients of spiritual workers. In March 1932, a forty-year-old spiritual worker named Pearl Harper was indicted by a Shelby County grand jury for selling a bag containing various powders to a woman whom Harper told could make her restaurant successful by using the magical sack. Harper's client purchased the bag and carried it with her for three weeks. After the woman saw no results from carrying the bag, she returned to Harper and asked for her money back. Harper refused, and the two ended up in court.

The mojo bag was also known as a "hand," "conjure bag," "cunjur bag," "jack" and "tobey." Several versions of bags were used throughout the Mid-South, each with its own specific ingredients and assigned purpose. Bags would be used to address gambling, luck, matters of love, protection and for their ability to break crossings. The following are some of the different versions of "conjure bags" throughout the Mid-South, listed by geographic region and ingredients. Newspaper accounts, historical documents and social commentaries have been used to compile this information.

Year of Documentation	Geographic Region	Ingredients
1877	Memphis, Tennessee	Lodestone, human finger bone and lock of hair
1886	Montgomery, Alabama	Lodestone, lizard tail, frog eyes, owl tongue, snake fangs, coon root, rabbit's foot and coffin nails
1889	Nashville, Tennessee	Left hind rabbit's foot, lodestone, John the Conqueror, red flannel bag
1891	Montgomery, Alabama	Snakeskin, herbs and tobacco
1895	Frankfort, Kentucky	Rabbit's foot, pair of dice, hair from a tortured dead cat, hair from a deceased African American's head. All these items are powdered and the bag is bathed in black cat's blood.
1901	Anniston, Alabama	Iron shavings, silver three-cent piece and lodestone.
1902	Clarksville, Tennessee	Nine needles, nail from a horseshoe and hair from a deceased African American
1903	Jackson, Mississippi	Human middle finger bone, bat wings, hair from a deceased African American

Year of Documentation	Geographic Region	Ingredients
1906	Natchez, Mississippi	Red flannel bag containing seven strings, piece of silver, graveyard dust, lodestone and hair from a deceased African American
1907	Arkansas	Dead snake, spiders, rabbit's foot, human finger bone and drop of blood
1912	Montgomery, Alabama	Powdered buckeye, black cat hair
1916	Meridian, Mississippi	Possum bone, hair, coal and iron
1920	Arkansas	White silk bag containing black cat bones, an arrowhead, various roots, white sand and a nickel

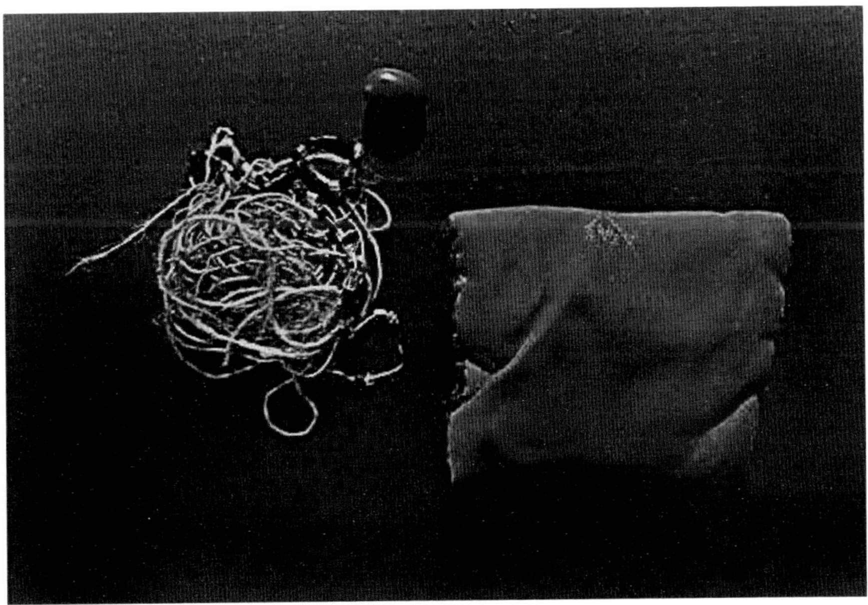

The "mojo bag" or "hand" was frequently worn on a string around the neck and in some cases under clothing to hide its presence. *Courtesy of author's collection.*

Bill Ferris interviewed a young lady named "Emma" about healing and spiritual practices in the Delta. The audio interview reveals some of the common patterns of culture found throughout the Delta and Mid-South. Ferris asked Emma if she had ever heard of a "mojo hand." She replied: "A mojo, it be something in a sack. And a black cat bone? You kill a black cat and get that bone, sew it up in a sack and that's you know that's called a hand. You can win anything you want, you can win money or anything you want, like having the rabbit's foot, anything!"

She goes on to explain

> *A mojo make you have good luck, win money or anything. Like you wanna keep anybody come in and they fool with that hoodoo? And they leave out, you can just boil Sulphur in your house, or ammonia, all like that. You can get some kind of oil and rub it all around you for good luck. You can get olive oil and some kind of else oil that can make you have good luck. You can just boil Sulphur right in the middle of the floor in a pot. If anybody suffer with hoodoo just put some Sulphur after they go, or throw some salt out behind them, table salt. That get rid of evil spirits.*

BURIED CROSSINGS

The fear of buried magical objects can be observed throughout the history of hoodoo culture in the Mid-South. As early as 1881, reports surfaced of buried or obscured objects that appeared to have had an effect on people who believed themselves to be targets of magical workings.

In 1881, Memphian Sarah White believed that a cloth bag containing hair and lodestone discovered in the fold of her mattress was placed there to cause her harm. The woman soon grew gravely ill and believed that the bag was affecting her health. The mysterious bag was eventually taken by White and a local rootworker to the bank of the Mississippi River, where it was thrown in to be destroyed.

West Tennessee hoodoo history is filled with accounts of mysterious bundles being left on people's property. And in many of the recorded accounts, the owner of the property demonstrates a certain amount of anxiety on their realization of what the object represents. *States Graphic* newspaper, out of Brownsville, Tennessee, some thirty-five miles outside of Memphis, reported in 1903 an incident in which a curio object was discovered, leading to suspicions of hoodoo practices. The article reads: "Julius Jackson, a negro living out beyond the graveyard was greatly wrought up Tuesday on discovering something inside his well of water. Investigation proved the find to be a small bundle containing pods of red peppers, dog's hair and a rabbit's foot. The negro is convinced that a hoodoo negro is after him."

Where did this fear of buried objects come from? Why were these rather mundane-looking objects the source of stress and anxiety for many in the Mid-South? The secret lies in the practice of southern African American conjure and even deeper in traditional African culture.

The role of the rootworker in the rural South was important to many African Americans who sought treatment for physical ailments. The herbal knowledge held by these specialists would help many families maintain health in situations in which there was little or no health care available.

The role of the conjurer was something different. Conjurers in the South had a great reputation for using various forms of sorcery. Naomi McPherson, in her article "A Question of Morality: Sorcery and Concepts of Deviance among the Kabana, West New Britain," defines sorcery as "a form of esoteric knowledge bestowing personal power which the adept can use willfully to realize desired ends." Throughout the Delta, conjurers were recognized for their ability to utilize esoteric knowledge for themselves and clients.

The conjurer would have the ability to resolve social stresses through various forms of spiritual therapy. Those perceived as enemies and oppressors could be combatted magically through the art of the conjurer. In some cases, the conjurer would operate as a spiritual mercenary of sorts, with clients paying for their services as a spiritual aggressor toward their enemies.

These services in many cases involved using material components such as charms in the form of medicine bundles used in crossings. These bundles would contain ingredients that emitted a form of magical energy that, combined with the creator's intent, could cause harm or the manipulation of situations. Some of these bundles would be hidden in the presence of their enemy in order to be effective, the belief being that by merely being in the presence of the bundle, the energy from the bag would affect the target.

A 1917 report from Montgomery, Alabama, tells of a practice known as "Loading the Pillow." The pillow is stolen from an enemy, and a conjure bag is inserted into the pillow. When the pillow is returned and the enemy begins to sleep, the conjure bag will make the victim suffer from pain in their head; this will begin to drive them crazy.

This form of contagious magic is one of the many hallmarks found in African-derived traditions. A number of African traditional religions have utilized these practices for centuries. In fact, in many cultures, the objects that are constructed and hidden may serve as "calling cards" of the ritual specialist. This can be seen cross-culturally among the Lolo people of Papua New Guinea. The objects are said to announce the presence of a ritual specialist, as they are discreetly hidden but are made to be discovered. As Marty Zelenietz describes in his article "One Step Too Far: Sorcery and Social Change in Kilengue, West New Britain," "In the dark hours, they steal into a village to plant sorcererized materials under a man's house, ladder or bed."

The practice of hidden objects as curses was observed by Sir E.E. Evans-Pritchard in his work among the Azande of southern Sudan in the 1920s. The Azande utilized a form of medicine known as "menzere," which Pritchard believed might be derived from an abnormal parasite. He describes the procedure that the ritual specialist utilizes: "The sorcerer goes by night, generally at a full moon, to the homestead of his victim and places the medicine on his threshold in the centre of his homestead or in the path leading to it." And, "Menzere is so potent a medicine that should any man for whom it is not intended step over it he will be ill for a while though he will not die."

Another example of this "hiding medicine" can be seen among the Igbo people of Nigeria in "ochuchu," in which misfortune or affliction may occur through magical means by air or buried concoctions in the ground. All that was needed was for the victim to either touch or walk over the hidden object. This was believed to be enough to magically attach the energy to the victim.

Considering that African American southern hoodoo culture was born from the root of African healing and spiritual traditions, it is apparent that many of the same stresses regarding buried magical objects continued, as well. Remnants of a surviving culture…

THE MYSTERY OF THE MEMPHIS NATION SACK

In the 1930s, Anglican minister Harry Middleton Hyatt traveled the United States, interviewing numerous devotees of hoodoo and African American spiritualism. During his stay in Memphis, Hyatt encountered an informant who told of a curious artifact: the "nations sack." Other local terms for the sack included *nations bag* and, probably the most used, *nation sack.*

Hyatt's informant shared that the sack was worn by females, typically around the waist. The sack contained money and objects considered to be "lucky." One practitioner shared with Hyatt that some nation sack owners would place parts of a chicken egg inside the bag; others spoke of adding objects such as roots, snuffboxes and silver dimes. One informant shared that some women included materials such as a dollar bill covered in their mate's urine in their nation sacks. Some were used in conjunction with a string that could be tied, in order to "tie" up a man's "nature," or sexual prowess. The magical principal was frequently claimed was that the ingredients in the nation sack could keep a man faithful and a woman protected. Hyatt's informant, whom he nicknamed the "Nation Sack Woman," advised the minister that the bag is off-limits to men and should never be touched by a man. She advised that the bag may also contain a "toby," a name commonly used in hoodoo culture to describe a "mojo bag" or a material object infused with spiritual power.

Hyatt notes that while the sack was mentioned in Memphis, it was virtually unknown along the East Coast and was rarely identified in New Orleans and Mobile, Alabama. Writer David Cohn, in his 1948 book *Where I Was Born and Raised*, shared his experiences in the Mississippi Delta, where he observed African American women wearing canvas bags suspended from their belt that contained money. These were called "nation sacks."

Blues musicians in the 1930s spoke of the mysterious nation sack in their songs and interviews. Robert Johnson's classic "Come On in My Kitchen" speaks of taking his woman's last nickel out of her nation sack. In his article "The Red Man and the Blues," Max Weber tells of how Memphis blues musicians such as the Memphis Jug Band's leader Will Shade noted that women who would collect money on the *Katy Adams*, a riverboat that transported cotton between Memphis and Mississippi, would place their money in small sacks known as "nation sacks."

Some writers, including Weber, allude to the fact that since so many blues musicians interacted with Native American culture and even spoke of the Indian "nation," this could explain the word *nation* in "nation sack." Weber also ponders the Native American concept of the "medicine bag." One cannot help but wonder if this influenced the nation sack concept.

There is certainly a precedent in African traditional religions for the use of charms and amulets in matters of love and protection. E.E. Evans-Pritchard mentioned observing the Azande people using various medicines to control social activities, from love to marriage and fertility. The use of medicine bags as a form of amulet can be clearly seen among the culture of the Bakongo people of central Africa, from which many scholars have traced many of hoodoo's practices and material objects.

There are a number of "recipes" for making nation sacks on the internet. Many of them utilize instructions obtained from Hyatt's interviews with nation sack owners. Some online esoteric shops sell "nation sack" kits to recreate this traditional folk artifact.

Some writers and academics have argued that the word *nation* is an incorrect translation of the term *nature* in the context of nation sacks. The language transcribed in Hyatt's interviews is said by some to have been interpreted through a somewhat ethnocentric view, disregarding the local use of "Southern African-American" accents. Others claim that the name comes from the shortening of "donation sack" and was used to refer to money gathered at church tent revivals or by prostitutes. The prostitute theory also claims that the money collected in the bag would "jingle" as its owner walked, signaling to potential customers that its owner was available for the night.

In her paper "Nickels in the Nation Sack: Continuity in Africana Spiritual Technologies," Dr. Teresa N. Washington truly frames the concept of the nation sack and its symbolism. Washington states: "A nation sack contains the spiritual and material implements of one's traditional and Neo-African identity. Those small bags filled with roots, coins, promises, hairs and prayers were tied to secret and sacred places, the womb or heart, where they recharged and strengthened the soul."

Regardless of what we call it, where it originated or where it was used, the nation sack symbolizes something deeply significant to all of us: the need for love, personal safety and personal success.

THE TRAVELING LUCKY COIN

A mysterious "luck piece" that showed up in a Mississippi courtroom in 1940 traveled some 150 miles through the Delta from the mojo city, Memphis, Tennessee. Rootworker Ed Bell had been arrested for selling medicines in the streets of Greenville, Mississippi. Witnesses came forth to testify that Bell was claiming to be the son of a well-known spiritual worker by the name of

Dr. Steward. Bell boasted of providing spiritual services for both black and white clients. Given attitudes toward race in this period, the fact that Bell would provide services to whites was considered important to segments of the black community. Bell not only sold numerous roots to his clients but also offered various charms. Roots were alleged to heal kidney trouble, while charms had the ability to bring luck and protect clients from danger.

One of the amulets that Bell sold to a client was a mysterious coin that was alleged to be able bring success. The coin was inscribed with the words "Good Luck, Love, Money" and "Happiness Kills Voodoo." The flip side of the coin contained the inscription "Lucky Mojo Charm." Strangely enough, this coin was created by one of the biggest hoodoo curio manufacturers in Memphis. Former owner of Lucky Heart Cosmetics, Morris Shapiro, created a "luck coin" that featured a man and woman kissing inside of a heart and the words "Good Luck, Love, Money, Happiness Kills Hoodoo," "High John the Conqueror Root" and "Magnetic Lodestone" on one side, and "Keystone, Lucky, Mojo, Charm" and various symbols on the other. The coin was promoted through ads in various African American newspapers that read: "Free Golden Charm Pocket Piece. Make today your lucky day. Just send your name and address and get marvelous magic Lucky Love and Money 'golden-charm' pocket piece, and big new agents' proposition. Write Keystone Lab, Dept. 6-J-8, Memphis Tennessee."

Conjure Balls

Garrard Harris, in his account of life in the Delta in *Plantation Life in Dixie*, speaks of the use of "cunjer" or "hoodoo" balls on the plantation. He describes a bundle made from a red flannel rag filled with horsehair, rusty nails, a piece of bone, a piece of colored glass and a feather. The presence of the ball on a victim's doorstep was believed to cause tremendous fear. Conjure balls were buried or placed on the property of the target of conjure.

As early as 1891, the discovery of conjure balls and similar artifacts were observed in the Delta. Sara M. Handy describes an incident involving the meeting between a spiritual doctor and a Western-based physician.

> *A prominent surgeon in a large Southern city, being called on to perform an operation for one of these doctors, and refusing a fee, jestingly recognizing him as a fellow-practitioner, was some time afterwards invited to*

be present at one of the doctor's powwows. "He made all manner of mysterious passes, regular mesmeric business, in fact" said the surgeon in describing the performance. "He scattered various vile-smelling powders on the bed and burnt a villainous compound in the room. I began to think I should be suffocated when he opened a window to let the devil out he said and then ripping open the pillows on which the sick man lay, took out several little balls of feathers which he said had done the mischief. These he wet with coal oil, burned them and buried the ashes. Then he announced that the patient should surely get well which he actually did, such as the power of imagination. However the fellow had a mild fever, and was much more frightened than sick and I believe the fraud was giving him quinine all the time."

Folklorist Joseph S. Hall interviewed several cultural informants in East Tennessee in 1956 who shared various accounts of lore surrounding witches and spiritual practices. Some informants claimed that witches in the region could be identified by their use of a conjure ball. A local witch was believed to have been identified when wads of hair were found in her straw bed when she died. The ball of hair was described as a conjure ball that would bring sickness or death. The hair ball was "just a little bunch of black hair mixed with beeswax and rolled into a hard pellet." Hall advised, "The old woman tossed this thing at the persons she wished to eliminate."

A number of techniques could be found in Mid-South rootwork and conjure to keep away witches. One approach used in Arkansas in 1907 suggested placing a barrel of water by the doorway of your home to keep away these entities.

One form of the "hoodoo ball" used the head of a puppy (mudpuppy) placed in the victim's cloth and rolled in sulfur. A form of the conjure ball found in Ellijay, Georgia, contained dog's hair and rusted nails wrapped in a red rag. The ball was placed above the doorway to the victim's cabin.

THE TOBY

The "toby" is recorded by members of the Federal Writer's Project as being popular in Mississippi in the 1930s. The toby is said to have helped stop a conjuration that had been placed on someone. Ingredients found in some versions of the toby included the lining of a chicken's gizzard, powdered

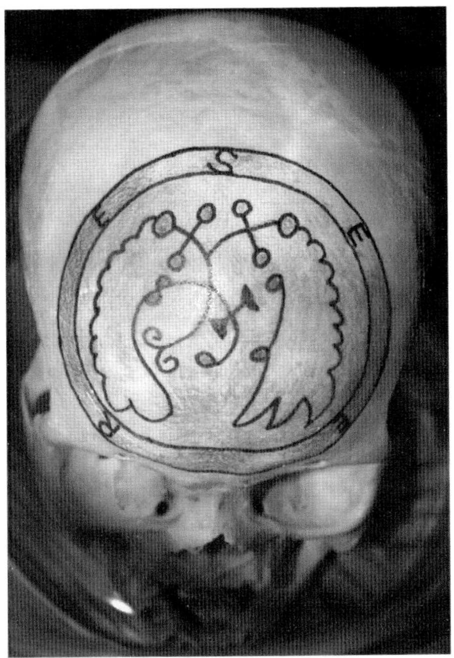

Left: From the collection of the late Doc Macon, this skull was used by Macon to consult spirits and discern the future. *Courtesy of author's collection.*

Below: Rootwork provided a means of survival for many African Americans in the Mid-South. Folklorist Newbell Niles Puckett documented these women using various curios and roots in their daily lives. *Courtesy of Puckett Collection, Cleveland Public Library.*

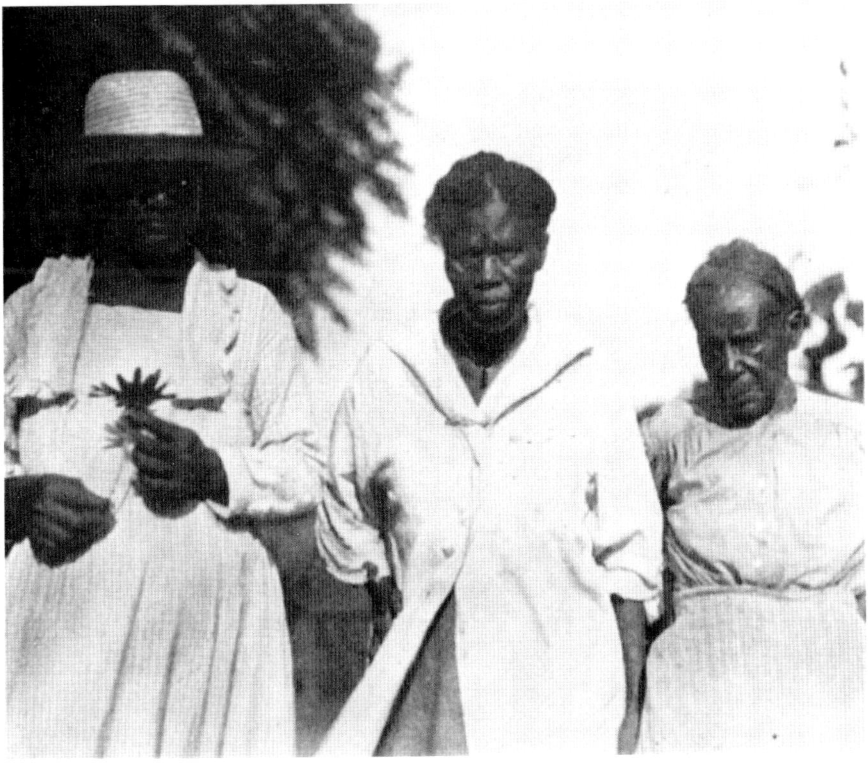

blue glass, pine resin, a rooster's spur and ashes. A variation of the toby found in the Delta, a "Three S Toby," was said to contain three ingredients that began with the letter *S*: soot, sand and salt.

Traditional Beliefs

There have been several incidents in Mid-South history in which conjure work was used to locate objects, including hidden treasures. In the late 1800s, a conjurer in Memphis known as "Doctor Thomas" was hired to release a spirit that was believed to be guarding a buried treasure. The conjurer met with a group of men near Manassas and Union Streets in downtown Memphis. The conjurer advised the men that it would cost them four dollars per person for him to perform his spiritual work on the guardian spirit. The owner of a local market, Crockett's Grocery, was advised by the conjurer to dig below an Osage orange tree behind his store. Mr. Crockett dug into the earth under the tree until he discovered a stone jar hidden in the dirt. Thomas told the men and Crockett that he would take this jar home after performing a spiritual operation and would divide the treasure and meet up with the men at a later time. Thomas disappeared into the night.

The following evening, the men could not locate Thomas. He had duped them out of their money and could not be found. The men enlisted the help of reporters from the *Memphis Commercial Appeal* to find the conjuring thief. After questioning several locals, it was discovered that a man by the name of Tom Lemon—"who is described as having a little red conjure bag with which he hoodooes the negroes or anyone"—was alleged to be hanging out by the Wolf River, where he offered his spiritual services to those who would listen. Following this lead, the reporters and victims discovered that this was not their man.

Local police were put in contact with a gentleman who knew of Thomas. Matt Stephens advised the police: "Doctor Thomas's way of proceeding are to see his callers in a dark room and when he goes home at night it is in disguise. And this way none of his customers know him by sight." Stephens and his partner had once hired Thomas to raise up treasure for them. The men had paid Thomas a combined thirty dollars, which had been obtained by pawning much of their furniture and possessions. The men never saw Thomas again and were advised that at least twenty different people in the neighborhood had been taken in by the conjurer. Thomas was believed to have been last spotted near the historic Elmwood Cemetery and later on in Chelsea.

In 1883, Mobile, Alabama police were notified that a murder had taken place in the north part of the city. A witness testified that the body could be found in a front yard on Clairborne Street. Police sent a detective to investigate the scene. The detective examined the yard, finding a raised mound of earth and a tin can filled with blood and a corn sack covered in blood from an unknown source. Police dug up the lawn, finding no evidence of human remains. Further investigation revealed that the yard was once inhabited by a woman who was known to have a lot of money. Now deceased, she was believed to have buried her riches in the same yard.

A neighbor of the deceased confessed to police that he had been in the yard attempting to find the buried treasure. He told police that in order to locate the riches he first had to "hoodoo" the witches who guarded the buried treasure. He expressed a belief found among some spiritual communities in the Mid-South that there are spiritual guardians that protect buried treasure. When questioned about the presence of blood at the scene,

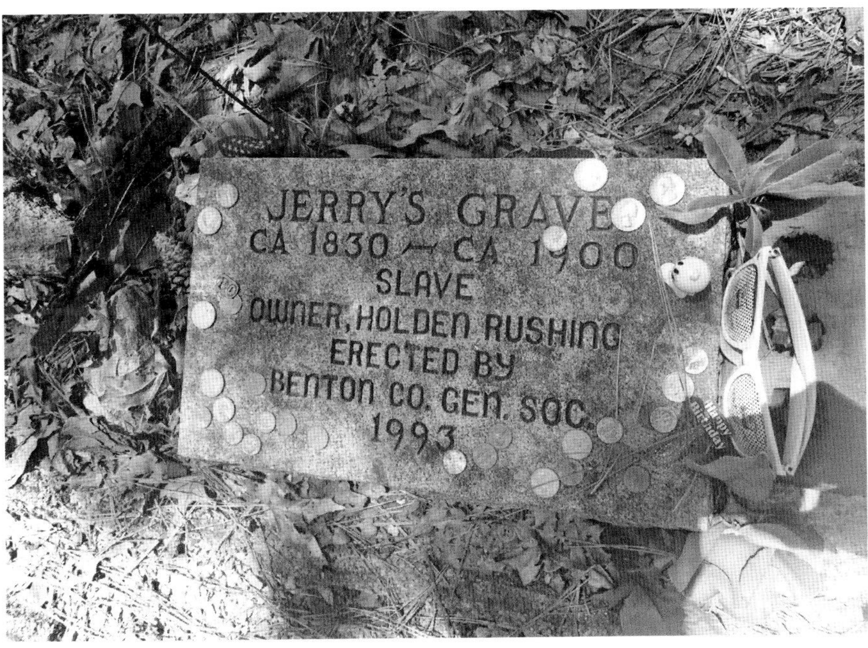

"Jerry's Grave" in Benton County, Tennessee. Jerry was a slave who was "given" as a "gift" to the daughter of a prominent local merchant. The grave site is frequently covered in gifts to his spirit. Someone attempted to remove his remains and left various animal bones around his grave site. *Courtesy of* Camden Chronicle.

he told investigators that while he refused to use his own blood to appease the witches, he had no problem using the blood of a chicken as an offering to the spirits.

One East Tennessee spiritual worker shared that one way to ensure the dead would not come back to haunt the living was to put the corpse on two planks of wood placed across two chairs. The body should be covered with a cloth and the eyes covered in coins.

THE PLAT-EYE

Spiritual techniques were used not only to locate treasure but also to combat spirits believed to be guarding buried treasures. Folkorist Newbell Niles Puckett tells of a spirit found in the Carolinas known as the "Plat-Eye" that has been described as guarding treasures. The same spirit has been mentioned in local folklore in the Delta. Puckett describes the spirit: "Generally the shape taken was that of a small dog (with fiery eyes) which grew larger and larger every minute. In one case hoofbeats were heard and a great horse passed by. Then only a little dog was to be seen. At other times these plat-eyes may float like wraiths along the marshes or unfrequented paths, or stoop like low hung clouds and envelop the victim. In another case a murdered husband's ghost hopped out of the coffin in the form of a frog, changing to his own form and going back into the coffin again."

Historian and writer E. Randall Floyd tells of the presence of the Plat-Eye in the South. "Plat-Eyes are evil spirits that come back to life for one of several reasons—to avenge deaths, to cause mischief among mortals, and finally to finish up tasks begun in life. Failure to give the departed a proper burial will also sometimes result in an unwelcome visit by the Plat-Eye." Floyd goes on to explain the possible origins of the Plat-Eye:

> *When black slaves arrived from Africa in the early 17th century, they naturally brought with them their own pantheon of spirts, demons and other creatures of the night. They may have been the first to introduce the Plat-Eye myth because of strong similarities to the ancient African belief that burying a person without proper rites will result in an angry visit from the deceased's ghost. To die without benefit of a funeral means the dead will be cursed to wander the face of the earth forever—or at least until it's banished through a primitive form of exorcism.*

He goes on to describe the various forms of the Plat-Eye: "As a rule Plat-Eye spirits generally resemble the bodies they once occupied. But they can also take different shapes—sometimes a dog or a car, other times a pig or cow or another human being without a head. Plat-Eyes have no natural enemies and will stop at nothing to terrorize a house, forest or graveyard. That's why such places—especially graveyards—are to be avoided at all costs."

Photographer Bill Steber, who has documented Mississippi Delta culture for several years, shared with me that he has interviewed men and women who claim the "plateye" can be seen in the form of a bull in parts of the Delta.

Haints

West Tennessee rootworker Miss Jessie spoke about a spirit that she would frequently hear knocking at her front door. She advised her children to not open the door, because a "haint" may enter the house. The term *haint* is believed by some scholars to have come from the Scots-Irish; others claim it comes from the Gullah Geechee people in the Carolinas, who descended from Africans enslaved in the Low Country of the Carolinas.

Folklorist Puckett defines haints as "unearthly beings who were at one time men." They are ghosts that live in graveyards, deserted houses and streams of water; on rainy nights, they prowl in the shape of a person.

Katrina Hazzard-Donald, in her book *Mojo Workin: The Old African American Hoodoo System*, describes the haint as "an evil witchlike supernatural being that is believed to chase its victims to their death or mount them during sleep and ride them like a horse until exhaustion sets in or sunrise appears. Haints are sometimes known as witches."

Signs of a haint include a black cat or a rabbit running across your path. Other signs are feelings of warm air and cold air. Some claim that you should never answer a strange voice in the night because it may be a spirit calling you. Lore found in Alabama teaches that haints will blow hot air on you, then cold air. It is also said that if you tell a haint your business, it will leave you alone.

Some practices used to keep away haints in the Mid-South included making a door facing out of new wood and pouring salt into your fireplace. It was said that the appearance of a little white dog meant that haints were near. It was also believed that if you murdered someone, you may be haunted

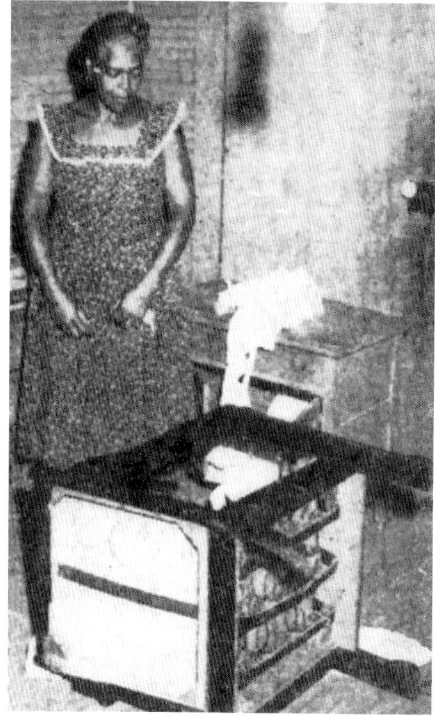

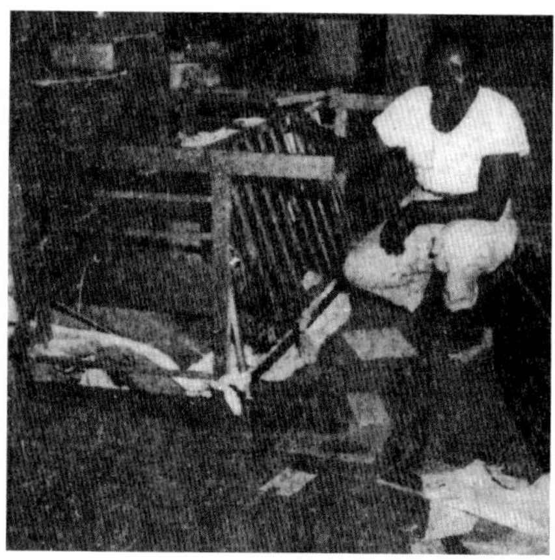

Above: Furniture tossed around the home was a frequent occurrence witnessed by homeowners and neighbors. *Courtesy of* Enterprise-Journal.
Left: Photographic evidence of a 1956 haunting that occurred in Fernwood, Mississippi. Local authorities believed it was the result of a "crossing" that someone had placed on the homeowners. *Courtesy of* Enterprise-Journal.

by their ghost. In order to protect yourself from the haint, you must place tenpenny nails in the pocket of the deceased.

Tennessee folklorists interviewed Jessie Lee Smith from East Tennessee, who explained that ghosts roam the earth till resurrection day. She claimed to have seen her first haint around 1900, when she was a child. She told folklorists that she passed an old dead tree and that there was a headless man in a black suit standing there. Blood was running down his shirt, and he was reaching out for her and her brother. She later found out that a man had died on that very spot. She also claimed to have seen haints in several different forms.

A spirit was believed to be responsible for a 1956 haunting of a home in Fernwood, Mississippi. Inhabitants of a house built in 1897 reported a number of bizarre disturbances while staying in the home. Willis and Mignonnia Smith began observing pieces of furniture turned over without the aid of human hands. The Smiths were alleged to have witnessed chairs, tables and even beds flipped over on their sides. Newspapers and pieces of paper would fly into the air and land on the ground, in front of the family's eyes. Sheriff Bill Andrews reportedly watched as a sewing machine was flipped over by an unseen supernatural force. Local police claimed that they knew who was causing these alleged paranormal disturbances and that it was not ghostly phenomenon, as postulated by many locals.

> *What is happening in Fernwood is nothing more than the practice of Hoodooism. Hoodoo is founded on the superstition of natives in the African jungle. One native may have another and hoodoo him. Often superstitions are so deeply engrained as to create a form of primitive hypnotism. This throwback to native African hoodoo is the basis of the chairs tumbling over the place in the home of that aged Negro couple. Everybody is talking about this new version of a haunted house. Sometimes one Negro will conjure another in order to get the victim's property.*

After observing the activity himself, the sheriff instructed the family to get their neighbors together in the home. Andrews instructed members of the Smith family to put all overturned furniture to their upright positions and warned the neighbors to put a permanent end to this "foolishness."

An account from Mississippi tells of a man who melted down two silver dollars to make a bullet. The bullet made of silver was believed to have the power to shoot haint-type spirits. Some spiritual workers were accused of sending haints to haunt their enemies. A court case in 1962 involved a seventy-eight-year-old woman who believed that a spiritual healer had sent haints to haunt her home.

3

HEALERS, ROOTWORKERS AND DOCTORS

I use the power of prayer, with a few herbs and ingredients to cure my patients.
—*Eugene Carey, Memphis healer*

Professor Warren and the War-is-Din League

The Mid-South has a deep history of spiritualists, prophets and traditional healers. One of the most fascinating personalities was Memphis-born spiritualist William H. Warren. Professor Warren combined elements of African American hoodoo and Eastern mysticism to create a spiritual organization for black Memphians that focused on personal success, magic and racial pride.

The War is Din Institute and Bible League (WID League) originally operated on South Lauderdale in downtown Memphis, then later on Vance Street. The name *War is Din* (pronounced "War isa Din") comes from the word that strangers used to call Warren while he was in India. Warren explained to a reporter in 1939 that the words come from the "Indian" words for "Wisdom I Desire." Author Shields McIlwaine, in the 1948 book *Memphis Down in Dixie*, claims that Warren told her the words were "Arabic." Warren traveled to India with a white physician whom his mother worked for in his younger days. It was in India that Warren claimed he learned what he called the "mystic sciences" that he brought home to teach to black Memphians.

Warren's spiritual practices included the use of candle magic and incense, roots and herbs, along with Christian and Asian religious iconography. He would use the Bible as well as playing cards to gain insight into spiritual wisdom. He advertised himself as a "Spiritual Adviser" and gave lectures about his beliefs, along with classes on creating spiritual art. He also conducted organized philosophical debates among members of his organization. Spiritual lessons were often taught during ritual dramas that reenacted biblical stories. Group "feasts," known as "War is Dinners," were conducted for fellowship, recruitment and learning.

Members of the War is Din community were divided into groups named after the months of the year. The "Januarians" were charged with taking care of fellow Januarians, and likewise for the other groups. Warren conducted individual and group sessions for his devotees that included lessons and advice on financial matters. Members were encouraged to save their money and not spend it frivolously, in order to further the success of the African American community. The cost to join War is Din was five dollars, with a monthly membership fee of twenty-five cents.

Potential members underwent strict physical examinations by a black physician and a white physician, as Professor Warren said he didn't want "bad disease" in the organization. Warren operated a savings club for member investments, keeping the interest from the investments. Members in various professions would use their positions as official members of the institute. For example, a member who was a barber became an official War is Din barber, dedicating his work to the organization. Members were encouraged to spend their money among War is Din official members, thereby keeping finances flowing within the organization. It provided health care for many of its members and even purchased medicine for them on occasion.

Professor Warren led classes in arts and crafts, encouraging members to create crafts using woodworking, as well as ceramic materials and clothing, to sell to make money for the group. He claimed to have learned secrets of creating artwork while in India.

Charity toward others was emphasized among the group. During the holiday season, members handed out hundreds of food baskets and clothing to those in need throughout the city. The organization changed its focus as an educational entity and began to call itself a "temple." Several black-operated newspapers, including the *Atlanta Daily World*, boasted of the work that Warren, "a noted spiritualist," and the temple were doing throughout the southern United States. Several organizations in the city of Memphis joined with the temple to conduct food and clothing drives during the Christmas holidays.

Warren's War is Din Bible League spawned several splinter branches throughout the United States in cities like New Orleans, Clarksdale and Chicago, as well as in Canada. In April 1940, Warren boasted of a membership of well over thirty thousand throughout the world.

In his personal life, Professor Warren married his secretary, Hattie Mae, who was known locally as being the 1939 "Queen of the Beale Street Cotton Makers Jubilee." Local media reported that Hattie Mae was crowned at midnight of the festival, and that as soon as her name was announced, Warren's followers began to sing a spiritual. A celebratory feast was held at the temple following the announcement. Hattie Mae and Warren took part in building the War is Din community over the years, including participating in a complex ritual drama at the War is Din headquarters. This included a play conducted over the course of the three days known as the "King Solomon Tour."

As Warren's reputation and influence grew in Memphis, he began to be noticed outside the black community. Some white-operated newspapers began to call him the "Father Divine of the South," referring to the scandalous black spiritual leader who once claimed to be God. National newspapers began to refer to Professor Warren as an obscure "cult leader," despite his gaining more than five thousand votes to be elected as "vice mayor" of Beale Street in October 1939. In 1936, the Department of Commerce produced a booklet featuring statistics regarding religious organizations throughout the United States. The booklet mentions War is Din as one of many "cults" that it avoided collecting data on, because it did not have "distinctive membership."

Professor Warren's kingdom continued to grow in downtown Memphis until April 1940. His wife asked for a divorce, claiming to a Memphis court that her husband had exhibited violence toward her and threatened to kill her. She also claimed that the professor was cheating on her with a new secretary in the temple. The issue of money was brought up in court for alimony, and Warren admitted that he had made more than $17,000 in a year from devotees' "Christmas presents" to the leader. Warren told the court that his wife had begun cheating on him while working with the Memphis Cotton Carnival.

As Hattie Mae claimed her own injuries and alleged that there were injuries on the husband, Warren showed the court an injury he had sustained the night before the trial. He revealed that as he was in his backyard feeding his dog, two men jumped out and hit him on the

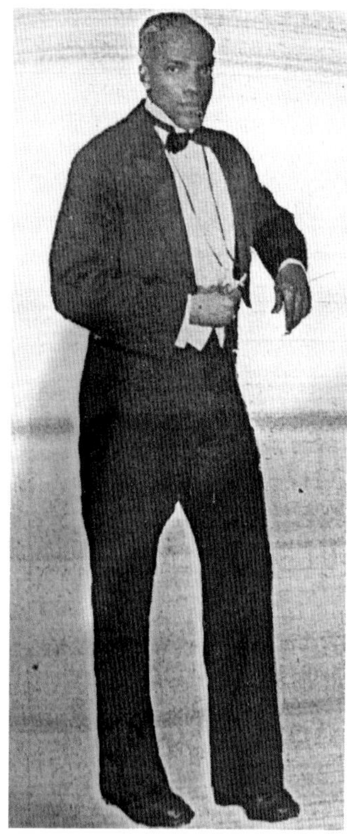

Professor William H. Warren, spiritual leader of the Memphis-based War is Din Institute and Bible League. *Courtesy of Shelby County Library.*

head and then fired a gun. The professor's attorney looked at the court and asked, "Do you believe this half-pint husband was cruel and beat this No. 10 size woman?"

The jury refused to grant Hattie Mae a divorce, saying there was insufficient evidence to prove that he had been violent toward her. Over 250 devotees of the temple showed up to the courthouse during the trial. Warren boasted to the press that there would have been thousands but that he had advised against that many attending. Following the judgement, members of Warren's spiritualist temple began to hurl insults, calling his wife "Haughty Hattie." Many of them told members of the onlooking press that she had been extremely arrogant and had been given a mansion, fine clothes and anything she wanted from the professor.

Professor Warren and his War is Din League disappeared as the aging spiritualist struggled with much of the negative attention given to his group by the press and local community. Yet he stands as one of the many examples of Memphis historical figures with ties to hoodoo and spiritualist history.

DOCTOR LYNCHA A. JOHNSON, MASTER HERBALIST

Lyncha Johnson was born in Bolton, Mississippi, birthplace of blues legend Charley Patton, in August 1883. Years later, Johnson moved to Memphis and became known for his work with herbal remedies. He took regional rootwork lore and combined it with information he had learned through courses he attended through the Dominion Herbal College in British Columbia.

Johnson created a line of products that he advertised through mailed advertisements. Many of them included prayers and spiritual wisdom from the doctor.

> *This comes to let you know I haven't forgot you. Dr. Lyncha A. Johnson, Herbalist and Naturopath of New Orleans, Louisiana, Wonder Herb Doctor, 372 Beale Avenue, Memphis Tennessee.*
>
> *Treatments on Installment Plan. Following are some of the diseases my herbs will positively heal: Epileptic Fits, Falling Sickness, High Blood Pressure, Rheumatism, Lumbage, Dropsy, Tumers, Syphilitic Rheumatism, Bad Blood, Diabetes, Asthma, Pellagra, Kidney-Bladder Troubles, Female Troubles, Gastritis, Ulcers-Abcesses, Catarrh, Pyorrhea, Nervousness, Stiff Joints, Shortness of Breath, Heart Disease, Paralysis, Piles, Lung Diseases.*
>
> *I have thousands of Herbs Barks Roots and Flowers for all kinds of diseases. I want all of my people who have been suffering for years for the lack of good medicine call and see me before it is too late. For behold my people are suffering and dying for want of attention, perishing for need of wisdom, knowledge and understanding of nature remedies and healing such as Roots, Herbs, Barks and Flowers. The Door of Opportunity stands open for you to gain your health before it is to* [sic] *late.*
>
> *My Daily Prayer: Oh God, forgive me of my sins and give me power over diseases of my people. And it revealed unto me, Son of Man, Ask me what thou wilt and I will give it to Thee. And I said "Oh Lord, God, My Creator, The Maker of All Things, Give me Wisdom, Knowledge and Understanding." And He revealed to me again: I will give thee the Eternal Wisdom that is Around my Throne. Go to the Mountains, Forests and Fields; Gather the Roots, Herbs, Bark and Flowers and use them. I will Counsel you concerning every sick and afflicted soul that will come to you, and you shall heal many. Have Faith and Be Faithful in every Deed. Yours in Christ Jesus for Health, Dr. Lynch A. Johnson of the Dominion Herbal College of British Columbia. Seven Days Old and Not Yet Born, I received Wisdom. Prices: $1.50, $2.50, $3.50 and $5.00 Per Herb Formula.*

In 1931, Johnson operated a drugstore in Vicksburg, Mississippi, on Washington Street. An ad in *Polk's Vicksburg City Directory* for Dr. Johnson's store offered "Thousands of Plants, Roots, Herbs and Flowers for Natural Methods of Healing." In the 1930s, Johnson became one of the many famous rootworkers on Beale Street. He lived at 372 and then later 488 Beale Street as one of the many rootworkers who took care of clients on that street. The local press spoke of how beautiful the doctor's home was on Beale.

In 1937, Johnson was arrested by U.S. Marshal Elmon Jester, indicted on charges of using the mail to defraud customers. The doctor was running a

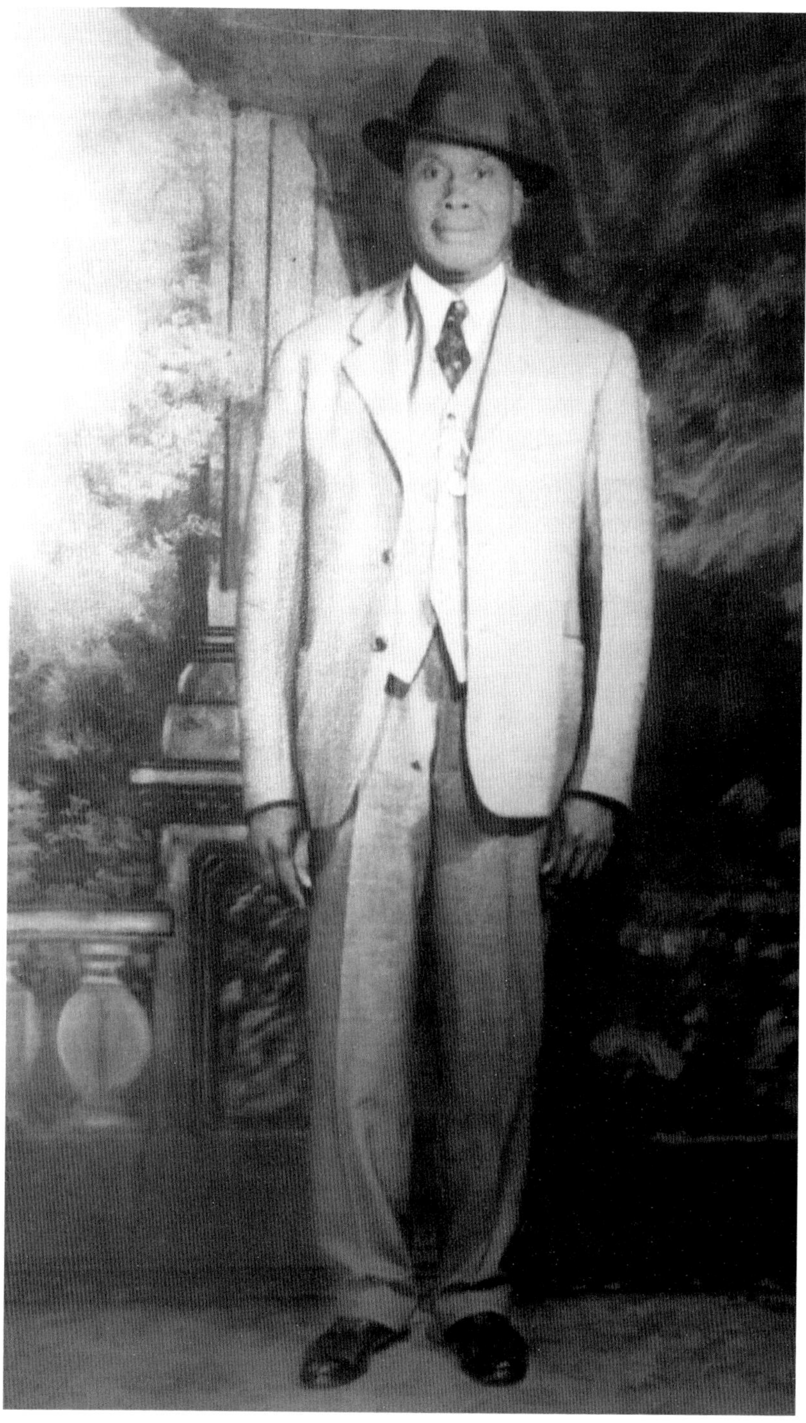

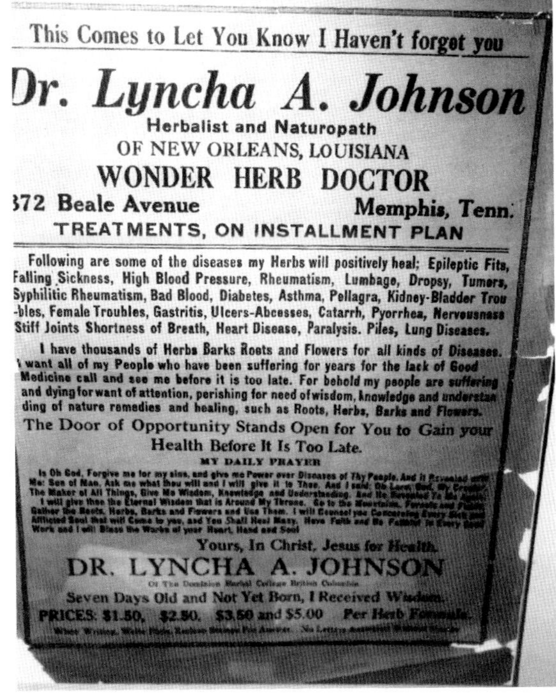

Opposite: Doctor Lyncha A. Johnson, spiritual doctor and rootworker of Beale Street. *Courtesy of author's collection and Memphis Pink Palace.*

Right: Dr. Johnson's reputation as a master herbalist from New Orleans gave him respect from clients in the Mid-South. *Courtesy of author's collection and Memphis Pink Palace.*

Below: Dr. Johnson sold many of his homemade treatments from his residence on Beale Street. Johnson ran into the law on several occasions during his career as a spiritual healer as a result of his herbal medicines. *Courtesy of author's collection and Memphis Pink Palace.*

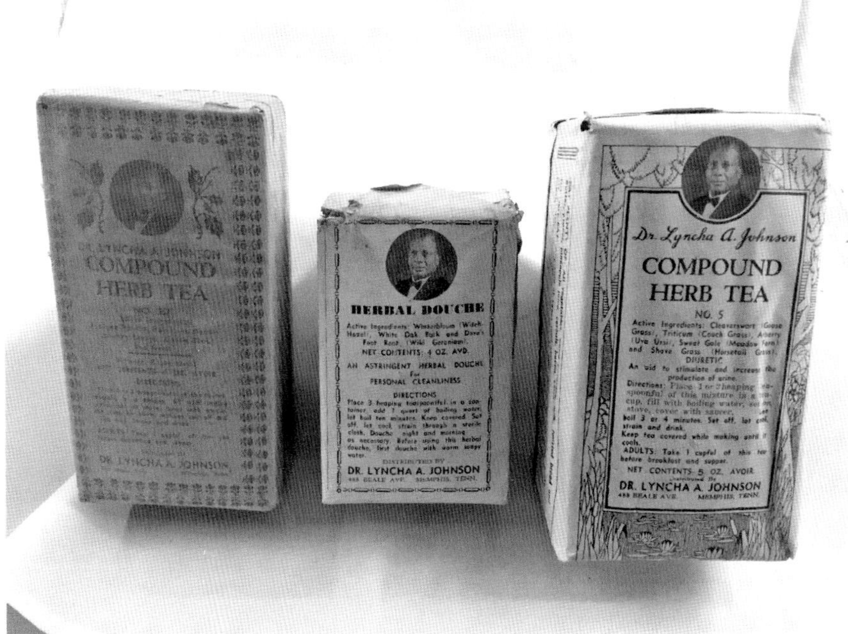

mail-order company in which he would mail clients the herbs they needed for medicinal and spiritual treatments. A complaint had been filed by a client named Louise Conner of Decatur, Alabama, after the doctor was alleged to have improperly filled a prescription.

Like many rootworkers in Memphis in the 1930s, Johnson had come under the scope of local law enforcement. Agents from the U.S. Post Office Department and the U.S. Department of Agriculture conducted an undercover operation to obtain herbs from Dr. Johnson. The agents sent a letter to Johnson, seeking help for a sickness called "Piazza" (which means "city square" in Italian). Johnson said he believed that the request for assistance was to help with "Psoriasis" or "Politis." Agents received packages of tea and a form of liver tablets. A lab analysis of the medicines revealed that they contained barberry leaves, prickly ash bark and wild cherry bark. The liver tablets consisted of ale, cascara sagrada and belladonna.

During the trial, 117 black and white clients of Dr. Johnson showed up, giving testimony of the healing work that he had successfully performed in their lives. Johnson had a tremendous reputation, as he was a member of the Bluff City Medical Society. His case turned out to be a mistrial when the jury could not agree on a verdict.

In 1938, Johnson advertised himself as a "naturopath" working out of his 488 Beale Avenue address. Two years later, he had a run-in with the authorities once again. The U.S. attorney for the Western District of Tennessee brought charges against Johnson for misbranding of medicines. The products were sold through the mail to clients in Arkansas and Missouri. The medicines that were said to be misbranded included some of Johnson's popular ones, known as Double Quick Liver Tablets, Compound Herb Tea, Blessed Herb Tea, Herb Wash and St. Bernard Compound Herb Tea. The judgement against Dr. Johnson read: "These products were misbranded because of false and misleading representations in the labeling regarding their efficacy in the treatment of ailments for which they were recommended: false and misleading representations regarding the efficacy in the treatment of a great number of ailments, including the most serious disorders: and in some instances because of false and misleading representations regarding their ingredients."

The government's analysis of Doctor Johnson's medicines revealed a number of components that, while they differed from the packaging, were commonly found in Mid-South herbal remedies. Herbs like ginger, senna, aloe, cascara sagrada (also known as buckthorn and thought to have medicinal and magical properties), mandrake and other ingredients were being used. Dr. Johnson's "Double Quick Liver Tablets" claimed to be "quick and strong on the liver," according to the packaging, but the authorities believed this was a false claim. The doctor's Compound Herb Tea contained such regional remedies as sassafras, chicory, red clover and other ingredients. The authorities again focused on the labeling. The label to the product promised to remedy "Whites, Gonorrhea and Leucorrhea," which were not treatable with this particular medicine according to the law. The Blessed Herb Tea, which contained mistletoe, couch grass, calamus and other ingredients, promised to remedy "Bloody and Scalding Urine and Stricture," a claim the government felt was false. The Herb Wash and St. Bernard Tea also comprised several regional herbal components but were not believed to be able to address the health issues promised on the labeling.

On November 20, 1940, the court found Dr. Johnson guilty and fined him $1,500 and six months in jail.

The legendary Doctor Lyncha Johnson died in 1946 in Collins Chapel Hospital on Ashland Street in Memphis of pneumonia after a month's stay. And while the courts may have argued his position as a healer, his death certificate lists his occupation as "doctor."

Doctor Moore

Jim Moore, known as "Doctor Moore," was a well-known African American spiritual worker around Copiah County in Mississippi. Born into slavery in Virginia, he was purchased with gold on a slave block in New Orleans. Frequently called a "conjurer," Moore was thought to be very proficient in both healing and crossing. He was frightened and respected by members of the local community, as they believed he had the power to kill someone simply by using his spiritual power. Doctor Moore was observed performing a ritual in which he removed a plug from a tree and would replace the piece of wood with a piece of hair from the target of his magic. Once the hair was placed in the tree, the target began to slowly become ill. When the tree began to heal, the target was believed to die. Doctor Moore could usually be seen wearing a bag on a string around his neck known to locals as his "conjure bag." After his death, a friend removed the bag from his neck and opened it to reveal a wishbone, a rabbit's foot, a button and some dirt.

BIG JOSHUA SCOTT

The city of Gulfport, Mississippi, was home to a spiritual worker known to locals as a "voodoo doctor" renowned for his supernatural abilities and his large stature. Joshua Scott, a large man weighing over three hundred pounds, was known for the many curios that he carried throughout town. His suitcase was said to contain such classic curios as hot-foot powder, stay-at-home powder, love powders, rabbit's feet, iron rust, graveyard dust and a number of lemons cut in half with small workings written on pieces of paper inserted inside of them. Scott was taken to court by a man who claimed to have been his client. The man had paid Scott thirty-five dollars to bring his wife from Chicago back to Mississippi. Scott performed a magical ritual, but apparently it was not effective, as the wife did not return.

AUNTY PAYNE

Another larger-than-life spiritual personality identified by her spiritual abilities and large stature was Missouri healer Racheal Payne. "Aunty Payne" was a prominent figure in the African American community. Payne weighed around six hundred pounds and was known for her healing abilities. Born in Howard County, Missouri, Aunty Payne was a successful nurse and spiritual healer. Clients would come for healing. Payne would pray over various foods and give them to clients. She would also pray over her clients for healing.

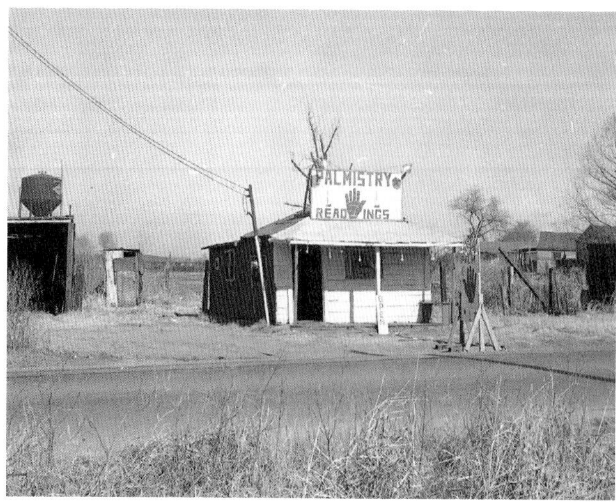

Some spiritual workers in the Mid-South stepped into the public eye and established businesses as "psychics" and "fortune tellers." *Courtesy of Shelby County Library.*

Local papers, including the *Chillicothe Constitution Tribune*, followed her work, reporting: "Aunty Payne, the well-known healer returned to her home in Chillicothe Monday. While here she treated a number of patients and Will Munn, who was bedfast with rheumatism when she began treating him Tuesday of last week was able to walk over a mile Sunday, down to Jim Campbell's and is feeling fine. Who and what cured him? On Friday, Aunty Payne treated thirty-six different persons for various ailments." Aunty Payne passed away on December 8, 1913. Local reports claim that the casket built for her was too large to fit in a traditional hearse.

Doctor Koku: Prophet of the East Tennessee Mine Disaster

In May 1902, an explosion erupted throughout a coal mine in the Cumberland Mountains of East Tennessee. The tragic catastrophe took the lives of 216 miners near Fraterville. The event would go on to be the worst mining disaster in Tennessee history. While local authorities believed the incident was caused by a buildup of methane gas from a nearby mine, a conjurer some six hundred miles away believed otherwise.

A few weeks following the explosion, an African man known as "Doctor Koku" began advertising his spiritual services to communities throughout New Orleans. An herbalist and conjurer, Koku provided spiritual workings in his cottage on the outskirts of the city. Dressed in a robe and turban, Koku delivered insight from African- and Asian-based spiritual traditions. The doctor advised local members of the press that the coal mine disaster in East Tennessee, as well as several other disasters throughout the world, were caused by a conspiracy of evil spirits.

Koku described a magical operation that he performed in which he interacted with a spirit from Zoroastrian religious lore known as "Ahriman." Ahriman, Koku claimed, was the manager of earthly affairs of Satan. Koku described an omen that he received that indicated something sinister was at hand in the spiritual realm. "During the day last Friday I went with my slave to your slaughterhouse for the purpose of buying vital organs of the beef which I desired to use in my experiments. Some of the men after having killed a fat steer, cut off his head and threw it on the ground. As I looked at it I saw the eyes open and the tongue lick up the dust. By my studies I immediately knew that this signified an undue activity of the evil spirits. In addition, as I sat at my studies the night before a dog from the street came to my door just on the stroke of midnight and howled."

The conjurer continued:

> *As I walked out to my lonely little house, I made a determination which meant much to me. I saw that the universe was on the verge of much disturbance. In my former experiments with the forces of the great Unseen, I had often called up the lesser spirits, Azealls, Montozan and others who acknowledged the sway of Solomon and many of the lesser demons who came under control of the ministers of Mahomet, but I never dared to call Ahriman, who is the head of them all and the most powerful spirit next to Satan. I resolved however to make the attempt though I knew I risked utter destruction. I fight against evil spirits and it is only fear of my power that causes them to appear and tell me things. I had been successful against all the lesser demons by using the incantations of the cabala. Against Ahriman I had but one hope—the Seal of Solomon which I found last summer on the shore of Syria with the help of my art.*

Koku goes on to describe the ritual in which Ahriman appears to him outside of a ceremonial circle drawn on the floor of his home. He describes the spirit appearing in the form of a red bull, a lion, a unicorn and a leopard. Koku demanded that the spirit tell him about the source of natural disasters taking place throughout the southern United States. The conjurer alleged that the spirit told him that spirits had conspired to attack humanity in various disasters that would eventually destroy the earth. Doctor Koku advised that he was in the process of preparing various amulets that would prevent the spirits from carrying out their plans.

Dr. Koku remained a fascinating figure in the local spiritual community until the local papers decided to do an exposé on his work. Reporters and a local medical professional visited the doctor, as he promised to summon the spirit of Ahriman and stop its work by the use of magical charms. The reporters were advised to take a "paste" that would allow them to be less anxious during the ceremony. The medical professional became suspicious of the paste and believed it to be a form of hashish. Sensing trouble, Doctor Koku advised that he needed to "cleanse" his robe from smoke from one of his visitors who was smoking a cigar. Koku would "step out into the moonlight" for this cleansing. As the good doctor stepped out the door, he disappeared down the road, never to be seen again.

The Nashville Spiritualist and Jimmy Hoffa

In the annals of Mid-South history, there are few colorful characters who can match up to the stories and hijinks of a spiritualist turned con man named Bernard W. Swain. Known as "Bishop Saint Psalm," Swain operated the St. Psalm Spiritual Church at 2520 Jefferson in Nashville, Tennessee. Swain and his family lived in the back of the church. The self-appointed bishop would perform healings and services for members of the African American community.

Bishop St. Psalm came under the watch of the Nashville police after it was discovered that he was making an alcoholic beverage and using it in his church services. His "holy wine," used during church rituals, was alleged to be homemade moonshine. He became known in the local press as the "Brewing Minister." The bishop was arrested for manufacturing the beverage in his church. He told the *Tennessean*: "I will say a special prayer for the inspector who raided me. I will pray God will bless him for perfect eyesight so that five gallons of holy wine won't look like fifty-five gallons of moonshine to him." Swain was fined fifty dollars in Nashville City Court. After being charged, Swain called together his congregation to announce that Lent would begin early with "a time of mourning with the symbol of death and suffering."

On January 13, Bishop St. Psalm did something that would define his work for years to come. Swain lay down in a coffin and announced that he was waiting until the Lord showed him what he should do about his use of holy wine in the church. Swain announced: "I am going into my tomb just like Christ. I hope to have God's answer about the wine in 15 or 20 days but if it doesn't come by then I will stay until I die." This was not the first time that Swain had used physical acts to protest what he perceived as spiritual dilemmas. Swain once spent three days attached to a wooden cross in protest of a student who had been expelled from a local school. Swain reported that when he came down from the cross he "preached a sermon that predicted a terrible disaster downtown. Seven days later the Maxwell House burned." The night that Swain entered his coffin, he preached a sermon in which he told the church he had a vision:

> *I was on a place like a desert and four lions attacked me. I picked up a golden sword off the sand and killed them. From the wounds came soldiers dressed like Roman soldiers, I estimate 10,000 of them. The Lord told me these are the soldiers of Satan who are descending on Nashville to make war on the Christian people. They are bringing sickness and confusion, making*

the churches war against each other, turning the races against each other. The only way to defeat them is to turn back to God.

Bishop St. Psalm would remain in that coffin for several days. In fact, he visited a local courtroom on a case while he was in the coffin. The coffin would not turn sideways to fit into the elevator, so it had to be stood up in order for the bishop to be able to travel in his holy casket. Swain became a frequent guest in the local courts in Nashville. On one occasion, he had taken a man to court for writing a bad check in church for $6.50. The bishop found out that the court costs would be higher than the check and dropped the charges. Swain became involved in a controversial scandal in 1964 during his stint as the owner of a local magazine called *Epic*. Swain approached two local high school teachers and alleged that he had photographic evidence that they had taken two female students to a local hotel. The bishop told the men that if they forked over the money for every printed issue of his magazine that could potentially feature their story, he would destroy the evidence. Swain told the men that there were twelve thousand copies of the magazine printed and that they would have to pay $0.25 an issue, equaling $3,000.00. Swain was arrested and charged with extortion. It was also discovered that several businessmen had become targets of the bishop's extortion rackets.

Later that year, the bishop became involved with one of the most notorious public figures in history. During the jury-tampering trial of Teamster boss Jimmy Hoffa in Chattanooga, Tennessee, a parolee working for the Department of Labor and Justice testified that he worked as an "agent provocateur" to "get Hoffa." The man claimed to have worked for Walter Sheridan, special consultant to Attorney General Robert Kennedy. "Under their instructions he told the court, he contacted Bishop St. Psalm, 'an alleged religious leader in the Negro community of Nashville' to ask him to use Voodoo on Thomas Ewing Parks, an uncle of Detroit Teamster official Larry Campbell. Campbell was a co-defendant with Hoffa in the jury tampering trial."

Bishop St. Psalm was alleged to have demanded that the Justice Department finance some advertising in his magazine. A witness claimed the bishop was taken to the federal marshal's office, where he was instructed as to what the government needed. The witness claimed the bishop performed a ritual using candles and a piece of material belonging to Thomas Ewing Parks. Agents were to be called once the target of the spell had been "fixed." The bishop told agents that, within a few days, if someone suggested to Parks that he was a "dog," Parks would drop to his knees and bark like one.

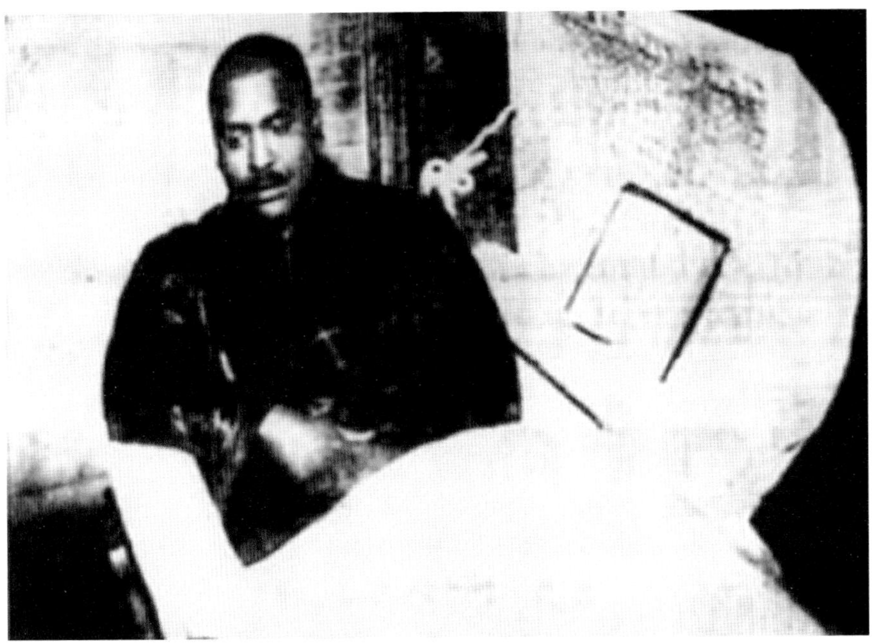

Spiritual healer Bishop St. Psalm waited in a coffin for several days to hear God after he was arrested for performing rituals involving wine in his church. The bishop later appeared in front of a judge inside the coffin in a Nashville courtroom. *Courtesy of* Jet Magazine.

The witness testified "that this action was taken with the full knowledge of the Justice Department for the purpose of 'exploiting the superstition' of Thomas Ewing Parks, so that he would testify against Hoffa and Campbell."

An appeal for one of Bishop St. Psalm's extortion cases was brought before the Tennessee Supreme Court in 1966. One portion describes the bishop's crime:

> *The presentment charged that the defendant had threatened to do injury to the business of one Johnny Beazley, owner and operator of Johnny Beazley's Falstaff Distributing Company, by instituting a boycott among the colored members of the community, and that defendant received from the aforementioned Mr. Beazley the sum of $3,000.00 in cash and a check for $1,200.00 supposedly for advertising in a publication owned, published and distributed by the defendant known as "The Epic," in order to end the boycott. The boycott, it is charged, was instituted under the guise of an organization called "The Nashville Business Men Association," of which the defendant was President and Chairman.*

Miss Sarah

Memphian Lula Reed shares a story about a neighborhood healer in the North Memphis Saffarans Street area. Saffarans Street was known colloquially as "Hell's Hollow" and at one time was home to Elvis Presley's family. Many early African American residents of this community worked in the fields and made their home on Saffarans. One of the most famous spiritual doctors, "Miss Sarah," was known for providing spiritual services for local residents. She could be frequently seen sprinkling green powder on her porch steps to remove any evil left by possible conjurers overnight. Miss Sarah was born around 1867 and could be seen walking to the funerals of strangers, where she prayed for the dead to keep their souls from hell. Miss Sarah attended a local Methodist church, where she was once overheard at a "watch service" warning attendees about being visited by a "messenger" with fiery eyes. Miss Sarah is a great example of a spiritual worker known within a local geographic region.

Doctor G.F. Murphy, Love Magician

As the number of spiritual doctors in the Mid-South began to increase, some workers began to specialize in a particular area of work. Some conjurers specialized in being able to get revenge for their clients. Some, like the infamous Doctor G.F. Murphy, specialized in matters related to love and domestic tranquility. In the 1920s, Murphy became known for his ability to heal broken marriages and to keep couples together forever. He had clients bring him a cloth belonging to the estranged spouse and performed a ritual over the cloth to set in motion a magical working guaranteed to bring back lost loves. Doctor Murphy came under investigation by the U.S. attorney, S.E. Murray. Dr. Murphy had begun sending letters to Memphians claiming that he had power to spiritually blossom marriages. During this period in Memphis, almost anyone claiming an affiliation with African or African American spirituality or traditional healing was in the crosshairs of local authorities. Doctor Murphy was placed in jail for four months, charged with using the U.S. Postal system to defraud Memphians. Murphy represented himself in court, where the judge was reported as saying, "Your endeavors to effect reconciliation are commendable but your methods are very, very questionable."

The King of Astrologers

Some spiritual readers in the Mid-South became very savvy in marketing their spiritual services. C.J. Mahundrew billed himself as "The King of Astrologers" and distributed flyers throughout the Delta claiming: "The King of Astrologers has arrived. Locates your stolen property and describes the one who stole it. Locates relatives and friends and makes home happy. Guides you in love, business, marriage and travel. Takes your birth date and places it with your Celestial Sign in the Zodiac and makes you happy. Locates hidden treasures and gets it. References any bank in the city."

A testament from a local leading law firm was printed at the bottom of the flyer as a form of endorsement. Mahundrew traveled through many African American neighborhoods in the Mid-South, offering his services. He offered "hands" that would bring power and luck as well as spiritual rituals to locate treasure and to draw success. Several families had paid the spiritual doctor, with little or no success. The King of Astrologers ended up in the courtroom of Greenwood, Mississippi justice H.H. O'Bannon. Mahundrew was charged with larceny and sentenced to seventy-five days in jail.

A Different Type of Rootwork

The rootworking and conjure culture among African American communities in the Mid-South has primarily been derived from African-based healing and spiritual cultures. However, there are also a number of non–African based forms of rootwork, healing and magic. Steve Crowder, in his paper "Black Folk Medicine in Southern Appalachia," speaks of three major folklore and healing traditions in the United States as Native American, European and African. All three of these have and do exist in many Mid-South communities.

As early as 1853, healers from these traditions provided healing and spiritual services for those in need. An ad for Doctor W.M McLane from August 1853 provides a good example of non–African based healing traditions in the Mid-South. McLane promoted himself as an "Indian and German Root Doctor":

> *Doctor W.M. McLane Indian and German Root Doctor respectfully announces to the citizens of Nashville and vicinity that he has returned*

again after a residence of fourteen years in the South, and permanently located himself in South Nashville, at the corner of Washington and Pearl streets, where he may at all times be found by those who may wish to consult him. He has in his possession certificates from men of eminent standing certifying to the permanent cure of thee most distressing cases of the following diseases—Nervous Affections, Liver Complaints, Dyspepains, Chills and Fevers, Plenristes, Asthmas, Colds, Coughs, Incipient Consumptions, Rheumatisms, Weak Lungs, Fits, Dropsies, Cancers, Ulcers, Scroffulous, Hemoptasis of the Lungs and other Hemorages, Diarreah, Diseases of the Kidneys, Mercurial and Venerial Taints of the Blood, Diseases of Children, Worms and other diseases incident to the human system.

During his residence in the South, he attended to over ten thousand different cases, all of which he treated with more than ordinary success. Dr. McLane hopes from his much experience in the Medical Profession and the degree of success that he has attended his efforts heretofore, to obtain the confidence and patronage of the sick and afflicted.

DR. J.S. ANDERSON, THE "CHOCTAW HERBALIST"

James S. Anderson, known as "Dr. J.S. Anderson," was known throughout East Tennessee as an "Indian" healer. Anderson, an African American man, claimed to be partially Choctaw and spiritually gifted to heal through the power of herbs. He has been documented as working in the coal mines of South Carolina, where he performed healings. In 1910, he appeared in a Whitley County courtroom, charged in the death of a child who had taken some of his herbal remedies. Anderson appeared in Kingston, Tennessee, around 1913 as an evangelist. It is here that he later advertised himself as an "Indian Healer." Anderson's ability to heal and prescribe successful herbal remedies spread his reputation throughout the United States. In February 1915, local papers recorded as many as eighty people a day coming to Kingston to see Anderson. Reporters noted clients coming from Illinois, New York and Texas, including some very prominent businessmen and women. A few months later, Dr. Anderson ended up in a Cookville, Tennessee court for charges regarding practicing medicine without a license. Anderson would continue to battle with the state Board of Health for several years as he established his own healing facility in Kingston known as the Choctaw Sick Home.

Anderson was an eccentric figure who also became known for chasing women. His wife divorced him, claiming that he was abusive and was seeing other women. His secretary became pregnant with his baby, and his own attorney advised him to stop womanizing. When he refused, the attorney stopped representing Anderson in court. Anderson was later arrested in Chattanooga, charged with drugging his secretary and raping her. This incident fed into the negative stereotypes of rootworkers, as newspapers wrote on the incident with an obvious racial bias. A 1917 issue of the *Tennesseean* reported: "The case is that which Belva Goldston, a pretty Tennessee girl and a number of other white women have been virtual slaves of a negro 'herb doctor' who wielded an uncanny influence seemingly over white women with whom he came in contact." Anderson spent his final days in Somerset, Kentucky, where he passed away in 1919. In 1926, a woman claiming to be his secretary began selling "Dr. Anderson's Indian Herb Tonic" in pharmacies and newspaper ads in Tennessee and Kentucky.

Paschal Beverly Randolph: Spiritualist Royalty

European-based spiritualist churches and later predominantly black New Orleans–based spiritualist churches both had a presence in the Mid-South. One of the most fascinating historically significant personalities who spent some time in the region had a unique grasp on both European and African American spiritual cultures. The famed African American occultist Paschal Beverly Randolph is a legendary figure among students of the esoteric and religious academics. Randolph was a physician, spiritualist, mystic and writer. He is credited with bringing esoteric teachings to the United States and organizing a number of religious and philosophical orders in America.

In 1855, Paschal Beverly Randolph returned from a number of voyages throughout Europe and Africa. During his journeys, he was exposed to diverse folk practices and spiritual teachings. Randolph became a "trance medium" and advertised his abilities in various Spiritualist publications. He became very proactive in speaking out against slavery and worked to help educate freed slaves in cities like New Orleans. Randolph would go on to form a Rosicrucian organization known as the Fraternitas Rosae Crucis in San Francisco in 1858. The lodge is still active and is the oldest Rosicrucian lodge in the United States.

He is credited by many researchers as being responsible for bringing the practice of esoteric "sex magic" to the United States. Randolph authored a number of books that are still sought after by contemporary esoteric practitioners. While his work focused on European-based spiritual practices, Randolph did mention African and African American traditions such as vodou and hoodoo in some of his writings. In his book *Seeership*, Randolph speaks of his encounters with vodou both in New Orleans and Long Island. He goes on to speak on the Mid-South through his citing of an article titled "Voudooism—African Fetich Worship among the Memphis Negroes" found in the *Memphis Appeal*:

> *The word Hoodoo, or Voudoo, is one of the names used in the different African dialects for the practice of the mysteries of the Obi (an African word signifying a species of sorcery and witchcraft common among the worshippers of the fetish). In the West Indies the word "Obi" is universally used to designate the priests or practices of this art, who are called "Obi" men and "Obi" women. In the southern portion of the United States—Louisiana, Alabama, Mississippi, South Carolina and Georgia—where the same rites are extensively practiced among the negroes, and where, under the humanizing and Christianzing influence of the blessed state of freedom and idleness in which they now exist and are encouraged by the Freedmen's Bureau, the religion is rapidly spreading. It goes under the name of Voudooism or Hoodooism.*
>
> *The practicers of the art, who are always native Africans, are called hoodoo men or women, and are held in great dread by the negroes, who apply to them for the cure of diseases, to obtain revenge for injuries, and to discover and punish their enemies. The mode of operations is to prepare a fetich, which being placed near or in the dwelling of the person to be worked upon (under the doorstep, or in any snug portion of the furniture) is supposed to produced the most dire and terrible effects upon the victim, both physically and mentally. Among the materials used for the fetich are feathers of various colors, blood, dog's and cat's teeth, clay from graves, egg-shells, beads, and broken bits of glass. The clay is made into a ball with hair and rags, bound with twine, with feathers, human, alligators' or dogs' teeth, so arranged as to make the whole bear a resemblance to an animal of some sort. The person to be hoodooed is generally made aware that the hoodoo is "set" for him, and the terror created in his mind by this knowledge is generally sufficient to cause him to fall sick, and it is a curious fact, almost always to die in a species of decline. The intimate*

knowledge of the hoodoos of the insidious vegetable poisons that abound in the swamps of the South, enables them to use these with great effect in most instances.

With the above as introductory, our readers will better understand the following, which we vouch for as strictly true in every particular. Names and exact locality (although we will say that it occurred within a few miles of this city) are withheld at the request of the lady, whom we will call Mrs. A.: "Some months since the only child, a little daughter of Mrs. A., who had been left a widow by the war, was taken ill with what was then thought a slow malarious fever. The family physician was called in and prescribed for her, but in spite of his attentions she grew gradually worse and seemed to be slowly but surely sinking and wasting away. Everything that medical skill could think of was done, but in vain. One evening, while Mrs. A. was watching by the bedside of the little sufferer, an old negro woman, who had been many years in the family, expressed her belief that the child had been 'hoodooed.' Mrs. A. was a creole of Louisiana, and, having been from her earliest infancy among the negroes was familiar with, and had imbibed not a few of their peculiar superstitions. In despair of deriving any benefit from the doctors, and completely baffled and worn out with the peculiar lingering nature of her child's illness, the suggestion of the woman made a great impression on her mind.

In the neighborhood were two negroes who bore the reputation of being hoodoo men. They were both Congos and were a portion of the cargo of slaves that had run into Mobile Bay in 1860 or 1861. As usual with their more civilized professional brethren, these two hoodoos were deadly enemies, and worked against each other in every possible way. Each had his own particular crowd of adherents, who believed him to be able to make the more powerful grigris. One of these hoodoos lived on or near Mrs. A.'s place, and, although she was ashamed of the superstition which led her to do so, she sent for him immediately to come over to see her child. The messenger returned and said that Finney (that was the sorcerer's name) would come, but that Mrs. A. must first send him a chicken cock, three conch shells, and a piece of money with a hole in it.

She complied with his demands, and he shortly afterward appeared with the cock under his arm, fancifully decorated with strips of yellow, red, and blue flannel, and the three conches trigged up pretty much in the same manner. Placing the conches on the floor in the shape of a triangle, he laid the cock down in the centre of it on its side. He then drew his hand across it in the same direction three or four times. On leaving it the cock lay quiet and did not attempt to move, although it was loose and apparently could have done so had it wished.

After these preliminaries, he examined the child from head to foot, and, after doing so, broke out into a loud laugh, muttering words to himself in an African dialect. Turning to Mrs. A., who was all anxiety, he told her that the child was hoodooed, that he had found the marks of the hoodoo, and that it was being done by his rival (who lived some miles off, although considered in the same neighborhood), and that he (Finney) intended to show him that he could not come into his district hoodooing without his permission. He then called the servants and everyone about the place up and ordered them to appear one by one before him. So great was the respect and terror with which they regarded him, that, although many of them obviously did so with reluctance, not one failed to obey the summons. He regarded each one closely and minutely and asked if he or she had seen either a strange rooster, dog, or cat around the house in the past few days; to which questions they made various answers. The chambermaid, who attended on the room in which the child lay, was one of those who were particularly reluctant to appear before him or to answer his questions. He remarked this and grinning so as to show his sharply filed teeth nearly from ear to ear, he said, 'Ha, gal, better me find you out than the buckra!' This was late at night, and, after making his 'reconnoisance,' he picked up his conches and the cock, and prepared to go, telling Mrs. A. to move the little sufferer into another room and bed. Promising that he would be back early in the morning, he left the house.

At an early hour next morning he returned with a large bundle of herbs, which, with peculiar incantations, he made into a bath, into which he placed the child, and from that hour it began to recover rapidly. He however, did not stop here. He determined to find out the hoodoo, and how it had been used; so, after asking permission, he ripped open the pillows, and the bed in which the child had lain, and therein he found and brought forth a lot of fetiches made of feathers bound together in the most fantastic forms, which he gave to Mrs. A., telling her to burn them in the fire, and to watch the chambermaid carefully, saying that as they had burned and shrivelled up, so she would shrivel up. The girl, who had displayed from the first the most intense uneasiness, was listening at the keyhole of an adjoining room, and heard these injunction. With a scream she rushed into the room, and, dropping on her knees at Mrs. A.'s feet, implored her not to burn the fetiches, promising, if she would not, to make a clean confession of her guilt.

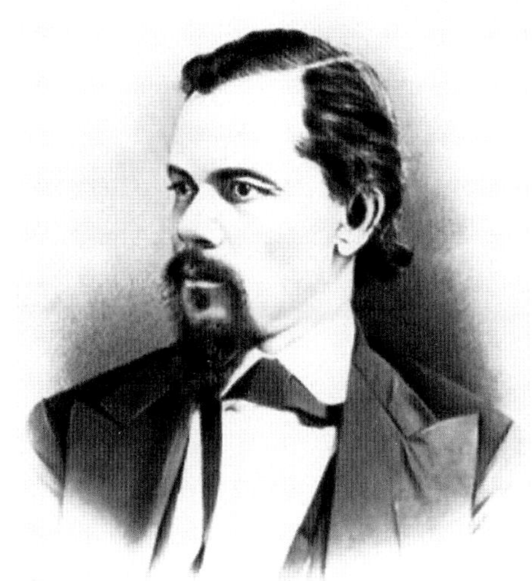

The Mid-South became home to many influential spiritualists, including Paschal Beverly Randolph. Randolph established a spiritual organization in Nashville in 1874 known as the Brotherhood of Eulis. *Public domain.*

Mrs. A., by this time deeply impressed with the strangeness and mystery of the affair, was prevailed upon by the entreaties of the girl, and kept the 'fetiches' intact, and the chambermaid confessed that she had been prevailed upon by the other 'hoodoo man' to place these fetiches in the bed of the child. She protested she did not know for what reason, and that afterward she wished to take them out, but did not dare to do so for fear of him. As soon as the family physician came in, Mrs. A., completely bewildered, told him the whole affair, showing him the fetiches, and making the girl repeat her story to him. He, being a practical man, and having withal considerable knowledge of chemistry, took the bunches of feathers home with him, and on making a chemical examination of them, found them imbued with a very deadly poison. Meanwhile, he told the affair to two or three neighbors, and getting out a warrant for the arrest of the malignant hoodoo man, they went to the hut to arrest him. The bird had flown, however, and could nowhere be found. Some of the negroes had, no doubt, carried word to him, and he had thought it best to clear out from that neighborhood. The little patient, relieved from inhaling the poison in her pillow and bed, soon got well, and Mrs. A. has now in her possession the fetiches which came so near making her a childless widow.

It may not be generally known to the public, but it is nevertheless a fact, that these barbarous African superstitions and practices prevail, and are increasing among the 'freedmen' not only of Memphis and Tennessee, but of all the southern States. It is the clearest proof of the inevitable tendency of the negro to relapse into barbarism when left to control himself."

Proved Oil Territory For Development

In 1864 Paschal Beverly Randolph, a seer attached to the Federal Bureau stationed at St. Martinville, La., wrote a book entitled, "After Death or the Disbodied Man." The 3rd Edition was published by the Randolph Publishing Co., of Toledo, Ohio, in 1886. On page 42 of said Book he says:—"Just like the mighty bay of oil now underlying the Parish of St. Martin, Louisiana. A body large enough and deep enough to furnish fuel to the world for a century."

Imbued with this faith we took an active interest in prospecting for oil, with the result that the Anse La Butte oil field is now producing oil and "Bayou Boullion" field produced oil at 320 feet.

Looking up the geological formation and the surface indications such as gas and ontcropping asphalt, we acquired large tracts for development i. e. at

Anse Anse la Butte..............(producing) 60 acres
Lake Catahoula............(gas and asphalt) 560 acres
Bayou Boullion ....(gas and oli) 4800 acres
Bayov Long.........................(gas) 250 acres
"Section 28"......................(gas) 1000 acres
"Cypress Island" ....(gas and oil) 500 acres
"St. Martinville.....................(gas) 500 acres
"Lake Larose"........... ....(gas) 1400 acres

We need capital to develop the oil in these, our terms for sale or lease are reasonable. All these lands are accessible within a mile by rail and water.

For further information write

MARTIN & SON,

St. Martinville, La.

Following several spiritual predictions by Paschal Beverly Randolph regarding a large oil supply underneath a Louisiana parish, the Martin & Son Company began to establish digs based on the seer's information. *Courtesy of the* Weekly Messenger.

Randolph criticized the doctor featured in the story, saying that his assessment regarding a "poison" on the object was a sham and that the operation had more to do with "magnetism" and less about poison. Randolph would go on to not only write about Tennessee but also come to live there in the late 1800s. Randolph's work in the Mid-South could be seen in his creation of a spiritual organization known as the "Brotherhood of Eulis" in the Music City in March 1874. He would write: "In March of 1874, I organized a society, provisionally, down in Tennessee. The B.O.E. to which it was my intention to teach all the occult branches of esoteric knowledge, constitute it my literary heir, and through it spring many lofty truths upon the world." He eventually went on to dissolve the organization and became a legend in the world of esoteric studies.

In 1864, Paschal Beverly Randolph had a vision in which he was shown that there was oil under the Parish of St. Martin, Louisiana. Randolph shared this vision in his book *After Death or the Disembodied Man*. In the book, he claims, "Just like the mighty bay of oil now underlying the Parish of St. Martin Louisiana. A body large enough and deep enough to furnish fuel to the world for a century." The Martin & Son Company of St. Martinville, Louisiana, began to prospect for oil based on his predictions and located a massive oil field in the Bayou Bouillon.

Years later, in 1954, a group of men were discovered using magical arts to locate buried gold in Raleigh, Tennessee. Luther Green, Joshua Harris and C.W. Cox were discovered with pine wood crosses, shovels, incense and brimstone on a cotton farm owned by Shelby Countian R.C. Crawford. The men testified that they had begun to dig for gold and were using the crosses to protect them from "haints," while the incense was used to protect them from "ghosts," and they were using "voodoo" to locate gold. The men claimed that a man who had formerly lived on the land told them that gold was buried on the farm. Brimstone was allegedly used to locate the gold. The men claimed that Harris stood ready with the brimstone to ward off haints and ghosts. The men were arrested but were not prosecuted, under the condition that they would cover up the hole they had dug during their operation.

4
STORIES OF THE ELDERS

Big Mama

The legacy of many Mid-South rootworkers lives on through the memories of the friends and families who knew these keepers of tradition personally. One such rootworker in the Memphis area was known as "Miss Bernice" or, as family called her, "Big Mama." Miss Bernice was born in the city of Moscow in Fayette County, Tennessee. Bernice told family that because of the immense amount of racism in the city at the time, she had to move away. Being young and anxious, she moved to the big city of Memphis, where she lived on Raven Street for many years. Her mother passed away in 1954, leaving her to care for herself.

Bernice had an ability to create remedies when anyone in the family or community became ill. For the children, she would combine turpentine and sugar to help with colds. She would take the grease from hog testicles and use it on injuries. Big Mama would frequently use poke salat berries and rub the juice into cuts and lacerations. She would advise family friends to boil white potatoes and place them into a warm bath for skin disorders. Her children noted that she kept a bundle of sage over her bed, possibly as a form of cleansing and protection.

Miss Bernice would pray for the sick before the morning sunrise. She would also use candles as she prayed for the healing of others. Like many Mid-South spiritual workers, she used the Bible as a source of inspiration

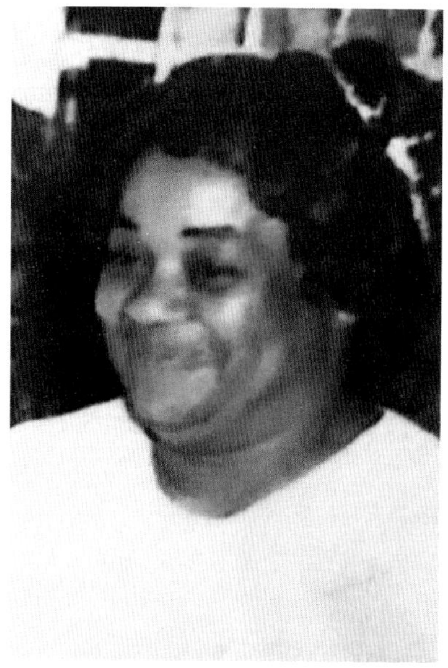

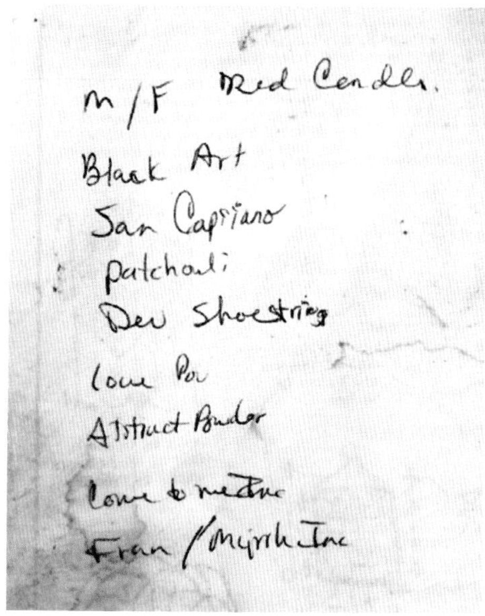

M/F Red Candle.
Black Art
San Capriano
patchouli
Dev Shoestring
Love Pow
Attract Powder
Come to me Inc
Fran/Myrrh Inc

Left: "Big Mama" Bernice Strickland provided healing and remedies for many Memphians. She would sit on the front step of her house and issue advice and treatments to her clients. *Courtesy of the Strickland family*.

Right: A shopping list of magical materials from the belongings of Mid-South healer Big Mama Bernice Strickland. *Courtesy of the Strickland family*.

and as a tool for spiritual workings. She was known for tossing a coin onto the pages of an open Bible; where the coin landed was where she would begin to read. She believed this was divine guidance leading her to a particular scripture. One of her Bibles preserved by her family revealed workings performed using Psalm 131.

Some say she could predict when someone was coming to see her. She would begin to rock back and forth and moan when she felt that someone was coming. Her family described her as fearless as she sat on her front step and told kids and adults in the neighborhood how she felt about them, good or bad. She advised family members about local folk practices, such as how to get rid of unwanted strangers by throwing salt toward them as they were leaving your property. She told the women in her family that the way to get rid of a man's unwanted advances or to do him harm was to place saltpeter and sulfur into his food. This would take away his ability to perform sexually.

She told her children to never let anyone sweep a broom across their feet and to never sweep into a house, but to sweep outward. (It is interesting to note that this practice can be seen in many Mid-South remedies and rituals. The sweeping "away" or applying medicines "away" from the body illustrates that "pushing away" spiritually.) As a result of what a broom could sweep away spiritually, she advised people to never use someone else's broom.

Family members recall various charms she carried on her body. She wore an example of a nation sack–type bag that contained coins and herbs inside of her bra, which she affectionately referred to as her "titty bag." She once created a charm by placing a dead frog on an ant hill and then taking the bone that was left as a charm. This is very similar to the process of acquiring and using a black cat bone in Delta culture.

She occasionally used mass-produced curios and books. Among her belongings was a list of magical materials that would be used in spiritual work. The list includes materials such as male and female red candles, patchouli, Devil's Shoestring, frankincense and myrrh, "Come to Me" materials, something representing San Cipriano and various powders. As one of the many spiritual workers who once lived on Beale Street, Miss Bernice left a legacy of healing, love and laughter.

James Andrew Heidelberg

Hoodoo in the Mid-South has primarily stemmed from African- and African American–based traditions. However, there are other folk traditions that recognize forms of healing and spiritual works that have found a home in the region. The practice of Germanic-based folk magic known as "Brauche" or "Pow-wow" originated among the culture of the Pennsylvanian Dutch. Spiritual workers of these traditions were famous for their ability to heal and affect change in the world around them. One such worker of this tradition in the Mid-South was a man known as "Uncle Andy" who lived in the small community of Mercer, Tennessee.

James Andrew Heidelberg was born on May 15, 1868, in Hardeman County, Tennessee. At the early age of ten, Heidelberg discovered that he had a unique talent. He recalled capturing a small bird in a trap. Before he was forced to let the animal go by his mother, he began to stroke and breathe on the bird. Within a minute, the bird gasped its last breath and died in the boy's hands. Astonished and puzzled, the boy captured another bird in a trap and repeated the same experiment. Immediately, the animal died as the boy's breath sprayed across its back.

Over the years, Andy, as he came to be called, discovered that he had a number of unexplainable abilities. He could run his hand over an animal such as a common grass snake and then blow his breath over the reptile; the snake would stop breathing and roll over on to its back. Andy struggled with his newfound abilities, even questioning what was wrong with him. Soon, he began seeking out snakes on the family's farmland, killing them with his supernatural acts.

As news of his abilities spread throughout West Tennessee, Andy's name became the topic of conversation in local households. Some claimed that Andy was full of "magnetism." Many West Tennesseans had no way to explain Heidelberg's power. On one occasion, he decided to demonstrate his power to a neighboring farmer. Ben Ellison watched as Andy cornered a snake in the cotton field. Andy ran his hand over the top of the snake and then blew. The snake rolled over on to its back and just lay there. Ben's wife, Mattie, shouted, "You conjured it!" Knowing that it must be a parlor trick of some kind, Ben raised his eyebrow in a skeptical smirk. Andy looked at Ben and said, "I will give you five dollars if you come back the next morning and the snake is gone." Ben smiled, as he felt the five dollars already in his hand. The very next morning, the men walked into the field, only to see the remains of the snake.

Ben looked at Andy in amazement. Jokingly, Andy said, "If you let me put my right hand on your shoulder you will know exactly how that snake felt when I blew on it!" Immediately, Ben's wife, Mattie, took something from her pocket and made a mark all around Ben, most likely as a form of spiritual protection. When asked by a relative how he performed these spiritual feats, Andy replied:

> *I can't tell you how I do it. It's just something in me. I rub the wart sometimes. Sometimes I just blow on it. But they go away. Fellow in Jackson had a thing on his upper eye-lid bout an inch long. It bothered him why he didn't have it taken off. He had it cut off but it would always come back. Nothing would help it. "Do you believe in conjue or hoodoo?" I asked him. He looked at me funny-like. "I believe in anything that would take this thing off" he said. I asked him then to let me blow my breath on it. He did and I blew on it three times. Two weeks later I went back and the thing was gone. He offered to pay me but I wouldn't take his money. "You don't have to wait for the moon to get right?" I asked. "Moon? The moon's got nothing to do with it!"*

The relative went on to say:

> *I've got a close friend who is also a "wort doctor." But his is done by a certain formula and when attending rites. The moon has to be right and he didn't come by it naturally. An old Negro so gifted passed it on to him when he died. Anyone who tells the secret has his powers taken from him, so the old Negro waited until he was at death's door before he gave it up. But nothing like this with Uncle Andy. He is a natural.*

I conducted an interview with Uncle Andy's grandson, who was very young when Andy died in February 1950. He told me that he remembered hearing stories of his grandfather's abilities as a child. He remembered seeing his grandfather remove warts with a simple touch of his hand. He also recalls that many people knew of his grandfather's work, but, like many Mid-South spiritual workers, he kept to himself.

Lynn Brown

In the early 1970s, teenagers around Greenville, Alabama, would take their dates down a bumpy dirt road to see an old wooden shack covered in kudzu. The old woman who lived in the shack was said to be a witch. They called her the "Corpse of the Kudzu Patch." On some nights, teenagers would shoot into the old shack, hoping to roust about the witch. The mysterious "witch" who became the subject of many urban legends turned out to be a traditional healer who performed healing works as opposed to curses and witchery. Lynn Brown was born in 1907 and lived in a wooden shack off of Ghost Road in Greenville with over thirty-five cats and a collection of medicinal herbs. Although she was not African American, Brown utilized healing techniques and remedies she had been taught by a slave whose parents had been taken from Africa. The young man's name was Aaron Coleman, and he worked on Brown's grandfather's plantation. Coleman was said to have lived to 116 and that, during his life, he and Brown became very good friends. He taught her healing remedies used by his family; in turn, she traveled all around the countryside, providing healing treatments for those in need. Although she was remembered by some as a "monster" as a result of myths and ignorance, she became known as an "angel" for the many she helped heal throughout her life.

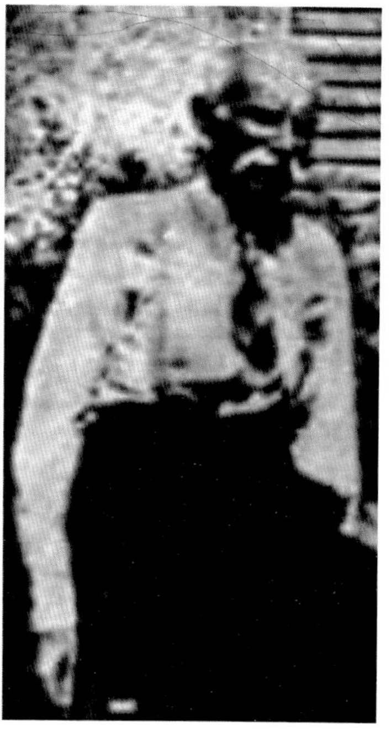

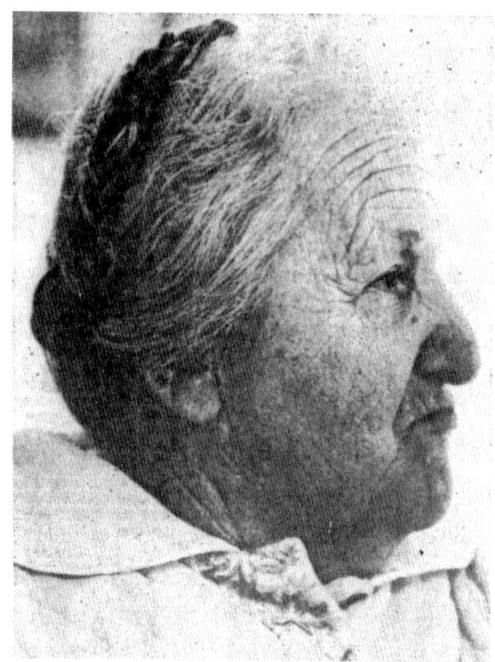

Left: A rare photograph of West Tennessee healer James Andrew Heidelberg. Known locally as "Andy," Heidelberg had the ability to heal wounds and remove warts by simply "blowing" on them. *Courtesy of the* Jackson Sun.

Right: Alabama healer Lynn Brown was given the nickname "The Corpse of the Kudzu Patch" by locals who did not understand her power to heal and work roots. She was taught healing remedies by the son of African slaves. *Courtesy of the* Alabama Journal.

MADAM GLOVER

One of the most memorable Christian spiritual healers in the Memphis region was known as "Madam Glover." Memphis pharmacist and herb man Dr. Charles Champion recalls his time with Corean Glover (aka "Madam Glover"). Champion had just graduated from pharmacy school in New Orleans and was selling various medications for his business. He discovered Madam Glover on the radio while he was traveling in Arkansas. She had a weekly show that she did from a local radio station, preaching and sharing Christian messages. She went on to work in radio ministry for over forty-six years. While working for Skaggs pharmacies, Dr. Champion connected with her and soon began running ads on her show. Glover would go on to minister to various churches and provide spiritual healing for clients. She frequented A. Schwab on Beale Street, where she would bring in a list of items from candles to incense for store employees to help gather.

Dr. Champion recalls a time when Madam Glover was having some health problems. She asked Champion if he and some others would pray for her. A Doctor Gatewood, who led a spiritual church out of Arkansas, drove down to Memphis to assist. He recalls that during the prayer she began to move about and soon was dancing, feeling full of life and energy. This is how he remembered her, full of life and energy.

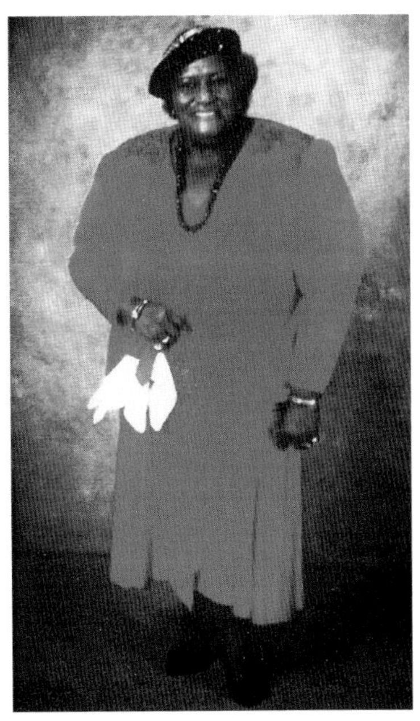

Born in 1918, Corean Glover, known as "Madam Glover," worked alongside Memphis pharmacist Dr. Charles Champion in Arkansas before coming to Memphis and serving as a spiritual healer. *Courtesy of the Glover family.*

In 1956, Glover led an Arkansas-based religious organization called Universal Spiritual Unity Union of Christlike Spiritual Churches out of Forrest City, Arkansas. Glover went on to form the Watson Universal Spiritual Mission, a home-based church on Walker Avenue in Memphis. After her marriage to Michael Watson, she became known in the churches as "Bishop C.G. Watson." In October 1973, she started the Saint Mark Ministries Church of God in Christ, which is still in service in Memphis. In her lifetime, Glover started seven churches. Madam Glover passed away on October 16, 1989.

5
THE BUSINESS OF HOODOO

PHARMACIES, SHOPS AND MARKETS

The Delta School of Voodoo

The term *voodoo* was frequently used as a pejorative to describe rootwork and conjure, with no regard or respect for the actual religion of Vodou. A 1929 case in Greenville, Mississippi, focused on the arrest of a spiritual worker alleged to be running a "voodoo school" throughout the Delta. Carrie Maxfield, a thirty-year-old African American woman, was fined and sentenced for practicing medicine without a license. Police stated that Maxfield claimed to be a "voodoo doctor" who operated in the area of Leota. During the court proceedings, Maxfield's suitcase, in which she carried her spiritual materials, was opened for the court. The report reads:

> *There were eight books one labeled "Silent Friend," books on crystal gazing and a marriage guide. In the suitcase there were voodoo or "conjur" bags, lodestones, horseshoe nails. Buttons, powder, several boxes of "Horsetail grass" which were used, officers say in the woman's voodoo practice. There were also in the satchel letters from all parts of the delta to the negro woman as well as from Arkansas and Louisiana. The school of voodooism is located at New Iberia, officers have learned.*

SPELLBOOKS IN THE DELTA

The discovery of the book *The Silent Friend* among the inventory of rootworkers in the Mid-South is a fascinating facet of the culture. The book, also known as *The Silent Friend: Marriage Guide and Medical Guide and Medical Adviser*, was one of many mass-produced books containing European-based esoteric teachings that were sold in hoodoo-related spiritual supply stores. Many of these books were published in northern states and sent to candle shops, pharmacies and spiritual supply stores in the South. *The Silent Friend* was published by the Chicago-based De Laurence Company, which produced a number of esoteric titles. The book was advertised as a "Guide to health, happiness and wealth" that "contains valuable information never before published, explains discoveries in philosophy and natural magic, gives secret recipes for making some of the best money-making articles of the age, steady income off hundreds and thousands of dollars." The book also contains information on constructing talismans and improving marriage and offers techniques for subduing runaway horses.

One of the most popular books in Mid-South hoodoo history is the *Sixth and Seventh Books of Moses.* It contains instructions on how to perform a number of magical operations, using detailed illustrations of various seals and symbols used to create change in the universe. Some researchers have called it the "black Bible," as it has been used in many African American spiritual traditions. Moses is an important figure, considered by some to have been, as Zora Neale Hurston calls him, "the greatest conjurer." Writer Patrick A. Polk says, "Taken together, the Bible and the 6th and 7th Books of Moses arguably function as the two most important 'conjure books' used in Hoodoo."

In 1910, the book was being sold in Jackson, Mississippi, by spiritualist "Professor" Charles H. Allen. Allen mailed circulars throughout Hinds County that read "Love, Happiness, Prosperity and Demonstrations of Dreams that Come True and the Meaning of Occult Science Explained by Prof. Charles H. Allen." Allen promised to send clients "Seals according to the sixth and seventh Books of Moses. They are said to aid everyone to success, love, happiness and prosperity if you observe the following instructions: To carry upon the person the first seal table of the spirits of the air who are quick to help as thought will relieve the wearer from all necessity." The circular describes additional seals and their uses, as well as their cost. Allen advised customers to wear "Two, eight or sixteen [seals] combined." Professor Allen resided on Pascagoula Street in Jackson in what was described as a very nice-looking home, and he had a local shop, where he offered many of his materials. Police arrested the spiritualist for using the U.S. Postal system to sell his materials. But authorities found it difficult to prosecute him, as witnesses against him were too scared to testify.

A 1924 case in Shaw, Mississippi, focused on the book's use as a guide by a local man. Equipped with the book and a compass, he was hunting for "treasure," which turned out to be a stolen car. The man told authorities that he was only going to borrow the car and intended to fill it with treasure once he discovered it.

Mid-South shops and suppliers would frequently offer the book and several other mass-produced "grimoires" or spell books. There is evidence that a number of spiritual workers in some very rural areas of the Mid-South kept copies of these books. Norman E. Whitten Jr., in his article "Contemporary Patterns of Malign Occultism among Negroes in North Carolina," writes: "Codifications of such beliefs were once used by white colonialists. Now similar codifications seem to help European superstitions remain with the great-grandchildren of their slaves and servants to whom these colonialists, consciously or unconsciously imparted their occult knowledge and rather specific fears of the unknown." Besides people traveling to shops and sales agents blazing a trail through fields and country roads, how did some of these books find homes in the rural Mid-South?

In April 1909, the population of Mendenhall, Mississippi, was treated to an introduction to Goetic symbols when Frank Lovell Nelson, editor of the *Chicago-Record Herald*, posted a fictional story in local papers about a detective fighting black magic. He included actual sigils taken from the famous European spell book *The Lesser Key of Solomon*. Tidbits and teases of actual esoteric concepts were frequently featured in newspapers and mail-order magazines.

Many European esoteric titles were advertised in newspapers throughout the South. In a 1923 edition of a Livingston, Alabama newspaper, a New Jersey company advertised "Original Sixth and Seventh Books of Moses with exact copies of over 125 seals, signs, emblems, etc. used by Moses, Aaron, Israelites, Egyptians, etc. in their astonishing magical and other arts including the period of time covered by the Old and New Testament. A book that should be in every home. Price $1.00." Elements of European ceremonial magic seasoned the literature and press of the Mid-South in the form of fictional entertainment and serious esoteric studies. Rural communities in Hattiesburg and Jackson, Mississippi, were exposed to the book *The 7 Keys to Power* via practically full-page ads in local papers promising "The Secrets of

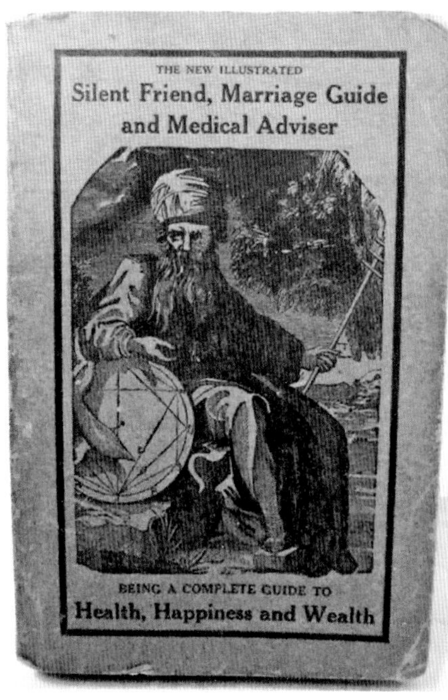

Left: The book *The Silent Friend* was one of several mass-marketed spell books found among spiritual workers in the Mid-South. *Courtesy of the author's collection.*

Below: Many spiritual supply shops in the Mid-South carried mass-marketed books inspired by European-based spell books. The availability of these books changed how some spiritual workers performed readings and various rituals. *Courtesy of the author's collection.*

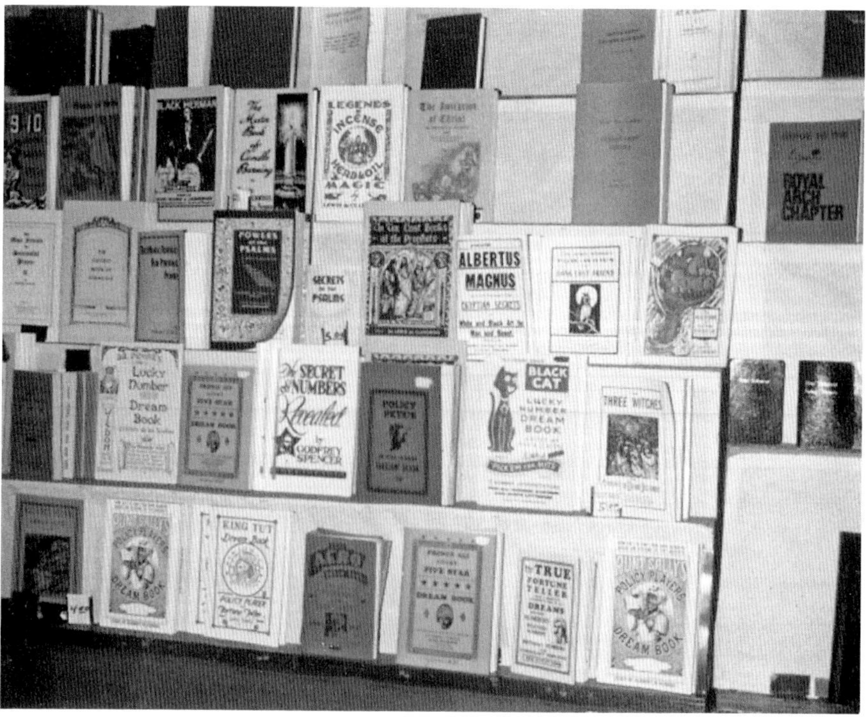

Ancient Forbidden Mysteries." Some spiritual readers like "Madam May" in Anniston, Alabama, began using these titles in their advertising, offering to teach the "7 keys to power" to clients.

One particular gambling charm was discovered in Nashville, Tennessee, by the local postmaster. The small chamois skin bag was on the floor in front of his desk. The bag contained a small piece of paper containing these words: "Ethura-Billibus, Jehovah-Deus, Father-Erad. I conjure, I cite thee through Jehovah as my power, hero, prince of peace. J.J.J." On the bag of the paper was written "N.R., Santus-Spirelolus, N.R." and "All this be guarded here in time and thence in eternity. AMICI."

The bag was eventually discovered to have belonged to a porter who worked at the post office. He had purchased it from a blind female conjurer on the corner of Gay and Market Streets. The conjurer was selling gambling charms that many in the community were quickly purchasing. The porter explained that the charmer advised him to speak the following words when he used the charm: "I breathe on the drops of blood, which I take from them. The first from their heart, the other from their liver and the third from their vigorous life. By this I shall take out all their strength, and they shall lose their strife in the name of God, the Father, the Son and the Holy Ghost."

The contents of this charm certainly drew inspiration from various European sources. The names and statement "Ethura-Billibus, Jehovah-Deus, Father-Erad. I conjure, I cite thee through Jehovah as my power, hero, prince of peace" are very similar to the contents of a table called "The First Table of the Spirits of the Air" in the *Sixth and Seventh Books of Moses*. The table groups similar terms as "Jehovah-Father, Deus-Schadday, Deus-Adonay. Elohe I cite thee through Jehova, Eead I conjure thee through Adonay."

Writings on the charm, including "N.R.," "Sanctus Spirelolus" and "All this be guarded here in time and thence in eternity. AMICI," are similar to a charm formula for protection found in the book *The Long Lost Friend*. That charm protects against evil and all manner of witchcraft and includes the same letters, with the correction of the words to "Sanctus Spiritus," or "Holy Spirit."

The spoken part of this charm—"I breathe on the drops of blood, which I take from them. The first from their heart, the other from their liver and the third from their vigorous life"—is very similar to a portion of *The Long Lost Friend* used to gain advantage of a man of superior strength: "I breathe upon thee. Three drops of blood I take from thee: the first out of thy heart, the other out of thy liver, and the third out of thy vital powers and in this I deprive thee of thy strength and manliness."

The popularity of mass-produced spell books and guides not only affected the practices of some rural rootworkers but also influenced how some curio manufacturers promoted their products.

The Memphis-based Keystone Laboratories distributed cosmetic products in the 1920s and '30s primarily geared toward the African American community. The company featured a line of curios in the Mid-South region that included incense, oils, perfumes and powders traditionally used in the practice of hoodoo. Many of the items were packaged under the label names Curio Products and Hi-Hat.

Early packaging of these products featured artist renderings of roots, horseshoes and other items commonly featured in curios from the 1930s. Two of the labels that appeared on incense featured imagery found on the covers of two very popular books in early American hoodoo history. "Old Aunt Dinah's Policy Players Brand Numbered Incense" and "7 Keys to Power Brand Incense" both featured titles and imagery taken from books that had become popular in the Memphis hoodoo culture as well as in magical communities throughout the United States.

"Old Aunt Dinah's Policy Players Brand Numbered Incense" took its name from a popular 1889 book, *Old Aunt Dinah's Policy Players to Lucky Dreams and Lucky Numbers Guide*. The book was used to interpret dreams and various omens that would reflect the number that the reader should play in the lottery-type game known colloquially as "the numbers." The "7 Keys to Power Brand Incense" reflected the name and imagery on the cover of the Lewis de Claremont classic *The 7 Keys to Power: The Master's Book of Profound Esoteric Law*. The 1936 book focuses on various techniques to master the future of the reader.

The use of titles and imagery from hoodoo-related books was done years before by the Valmor Corporation. Carolyn Morrow Long, in her classic book *Spiritual Merchants: Religion, Magic and Commerce*, tells of how the 1945 Valmor Products catalogue featured the same concept, using Claremont's *7 Keys to Power* and Aunt Sally's Lucky Dream Incense and Black Herman Incense from the book of the same name. Many of the items were sold alongside the book that they referenced.

It is fascinating to see how this trend affected the packaging of various conjure products. Today, Indio Products from California offers "Black Herman Psychic Oil" with a title and image that pay homage to the book. Internationally, a Nigerian company now offers an herbal medication called

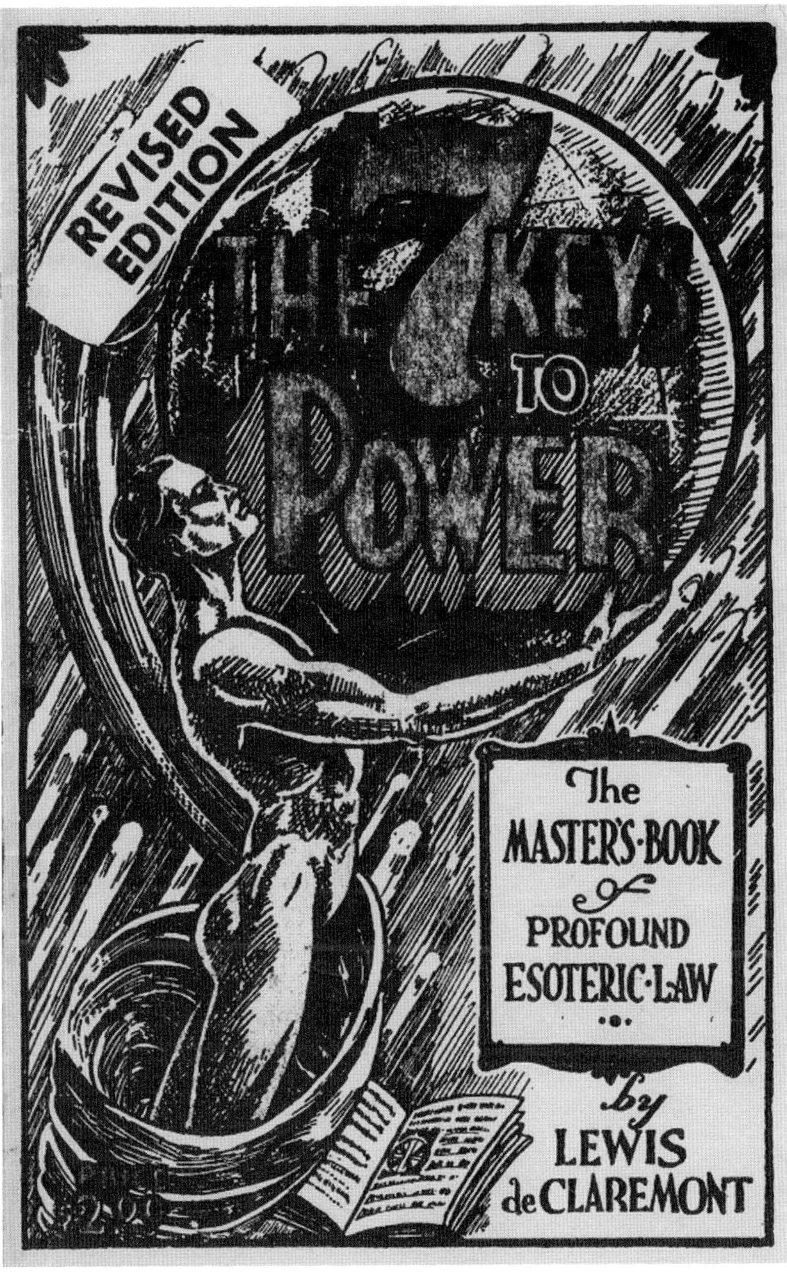

Lewis de Claremont's *7 Keys to Power* became a popular tome among conjurers in the Mid-South. It was available in many spiritual supply stores. Some curio companies like Keystone Laboratories in Memphis created incense using the name and aesthetics found on the cover of the book. *Courtesy of the author's collection.*

Aladdin's 7 Keys Herbal Mixture, which was previously called Dr. Aladdin's Seven Keys to Power and features a slightly altered image of the cover of Claremont's classic book.

Memphians in the conjure community became aware of many of these books through local shops, such as A. Schwab on Beale Street, as well as pharmacies and beauty shops that sold numerous copies of *Aunt Dinah's*, *Black Herman* and Claremont's *7 Keys*.

THE BUSINESS OF SPIRITUAL ADVISORS

Some of the interesting aesthetics that could frequently be seen in the Mid-South hoodoo culture were imagery related to "exotic" spiritual personalities. Traditional healers and spiritual readers began to appear with titles such as "Yogi," "Hindoo," "Indian," "Gypsy "Egyptian" and "Oriental." These titles carried a degree of spiritual power in the Mid-South, as it was the common belief that members of these cultures were perhaps more in touch with the metaphysical. The following appeared in an ad in the *Paducah Sun* of May 22, 1906:

> *Madamoiselle Ismar, Egyptian Palmist and Clairvoyant. A descendant of a race of people who have been clairvoyants for ages, her reading of your past, present and future life will amaze you.*

Palm readers claiming to be from "Gypsy Camps" were quite popular in cities like Nashville, Tennessee. Stereotypes of Hollywood "gypsies" were promoted to the public with claims such as "The Seventh Daughter of the Seventh." East Tennessee had prominent figures in the 1920s, such as Madam Allli Rajah, who claimed to be an "Egyptian Mentalist." Dr. La Rose charmed regions of Arkansas wearing a fancy turban decorated with the star and crescent moon. Some local businesses took advantage of the presence of these "exotic" spiritualists. In 1931, the White Way Beauty Shop in Hope, Arkansas, offered free spiritual readings from mystic reader Peo Del Marco for every customer who spent at least one dollar on hair treatments. Throughout the Delta, there were many spiritual personalities with "exotic" ties, like "The Egyptian Palmist" of Jackson, Mississippi, or a group of readers calling themselves the "Hindu Yogi's of India" in Natchez, Mississippi. They offered wisdom from the Vedas and "separate rooms for

CLAIRVOYANTS

50c--VEDA--50c

World's Famous Palmists
HINDU YOGI'S OF INDIA

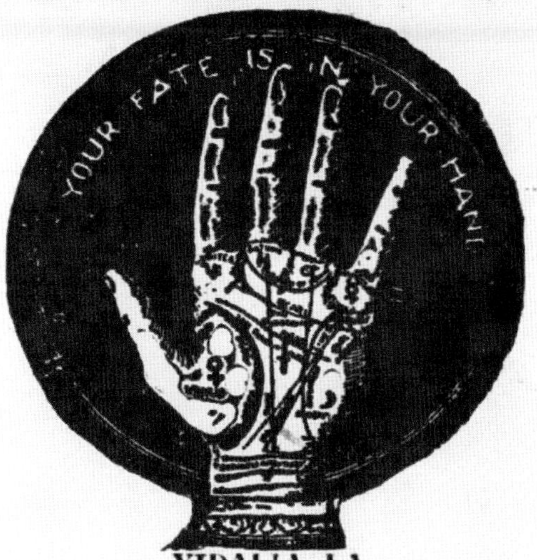

VIDALIA, LA.

After leaving ferry walk two blocks straight ahead, then turn one-half a block to the left—opposite Postoffice. See sign on house. Separate rooms for White and Colored.

DR. LA ROSE

THE HINDU SEER

CLAIRVOYANT

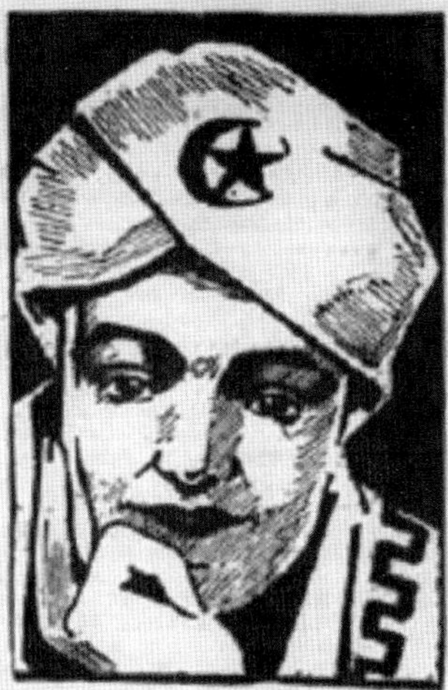

PRIVATE STUDIO
Southwest Corner (Upstairs)
Main and Market Streets
Jackson, Tennessee
Maid In Attendance

Opening 9 A. M. Today
Office hours, 9 a. m. to 8 p. m., daily and Sunday.

From towns, from villages, from hamlets in the state of Tennessee they are expected to come to see the wonderful demonstration of the great La Rose. And why not?

Twenty-three years ago Dr. La Rose graduated from the best occult college in the world, and since then has continually practiced his profession. I have the largest practice because I have had the most experience. Any person who needs my help may come to me in full confidence and be assured of perfect secrecy in my consultation. There is (or ought to be) some consolation in the knowledge that when you consult LA ROSE you have seen the best, and his fees are no higher than the charge of those less competent.

World's Supreme Clairvoyant

Above: An ad from a Mid-South newspaper advertising spiritual services of an alleged "Hindu Yogi." The ad reflects the time of segregation, as it advertises "Separate Rooms for White and Colored." *Courtesy of the* Natchez Democrat.

Right: An ad for Dr. La Rose, touted as the "World's Best Clairvoyant." La Rose was one of many spiritual workers who performed readings in Jackson, Tennessee. *Courtesy of the* Jackson Sun.

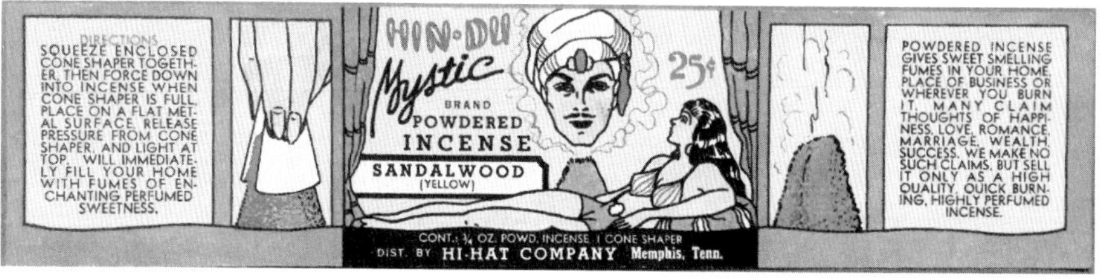

The popularity of exotic "Hindu" imagery in hoodoo culture found its way into mass-manufactured curios. This incense label from Hi-Hat out of Memphis featured a turban-wearing mystic to draw in customers. *Courtesy of author's collection.*

white or colored." Natchez also entertained readers such as Madame Koran, who claimed to be a "phrenologist" who could study the size and shape of a client's skull for insight into their personality.

The effectiveness of "exotic" spiritual readers was also considered in the advertising for spiritual products and mass-produced curios. Products alleged to have been "made by Hindus" were viewed by some as supernaturally endowed with power. Phillip Deslippe writes in his paper "The Hindu in Hoodoo: Fake Yogis, Pseudo Swamis, and the Manufacture of African American Folk Magic": "The words 'yogi' and 'Hindu' were used to describe a vast array of magical materials and a turban-clad wonder-worker was an unavoidable figure both in print and in person. Their ubiquity is not only an underappreciated phenomenon within Hoodoo, but it is also emblematic of the radical transformations that changed Hoodoo during the interwar decades."

Injecting themselves into communities alongside African American folk healers and spiritual doctors, "exotic" readers faced similar issues as those of their black predecessors. There were issues of racial hostility from the white community, as well as biased fears of "other" cultures. However, there was also a strange sense of acceptance by many in the white community of "exotic readers." A "Hindu Swami" reading tea leaves for slave owners at opera houses and local parlors was titillating, while African American rootworkers and African healers were looked on by many with disdain.

> *Hindu Hoodoo, 19, Cuts Negro Wife 22 Times; She Lives.*
> *May 23 1925, In a fit of jealous frenzy, Biminas Abdullah Rachallah Villiamalvoosh, 35, Hindu magician, slashed his 19-year-old negro wife in 22 different places at a negro rooming house at 408 Willow street, Saturday morning. The negro girl was taken to the General Hospital where several hours were spent in stitching up her wounds. She is expected to recover.*

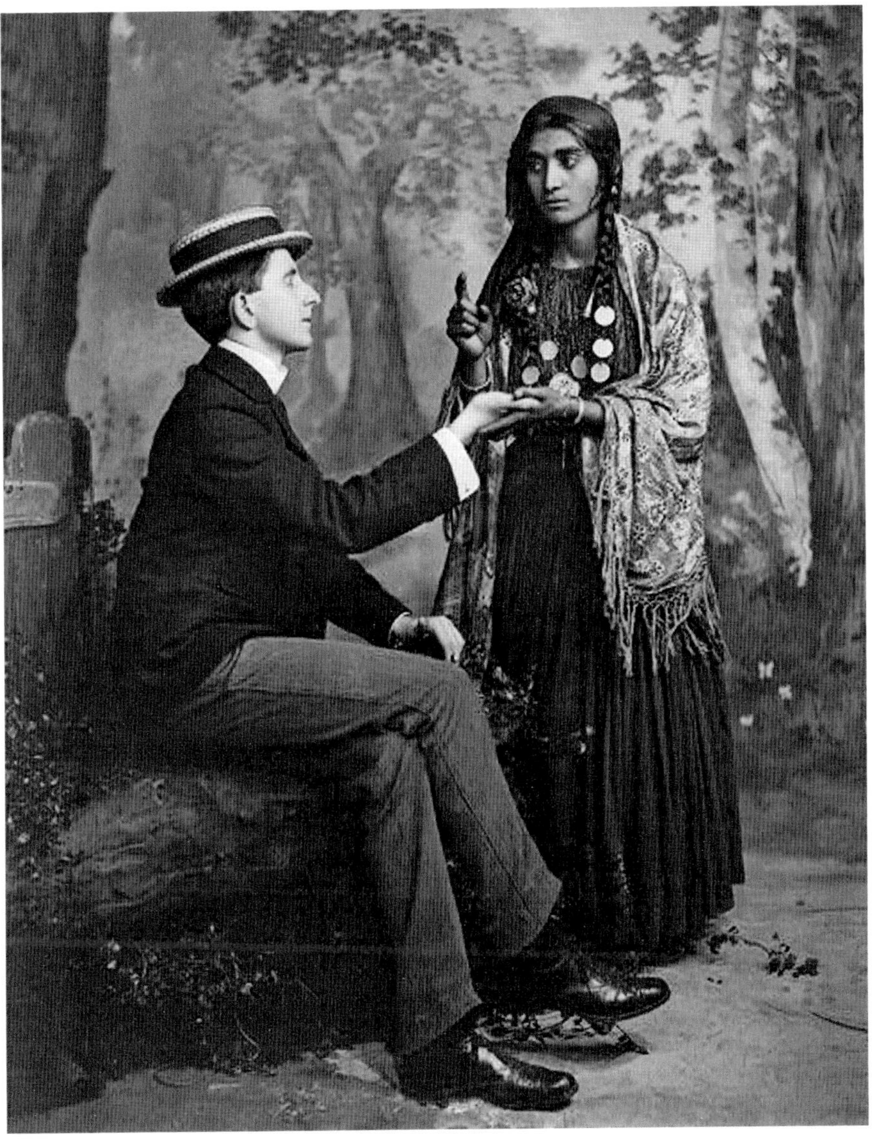

Spiritual workers posing as "Hindoos," "Swamis" and "Yogis" became very popular in the Mid-South Hoodoo culture. The appearance of the "exotic" brought an "air" of mysticism and authenticity to spiritual workers. *Public domain.*

Spiritual products and curios began featuring the imagery of "exotic" figures to attract sales. Mustached spiritualists with fluffy turbans were soon commonplace on the covers of sales catalogues and labels of oils, powders and incense. Curio manufactures out of Memphis began using these images. The "Magic Love" satchet powder from the Lucky Mon-Gol Company featured an image of a "Middle Eastern" landscape under moon and stars as a man with a turban overlooked the city. The Hi-Hat Company, also from Memphis, offered Hindu Mystic Brand Powdered Incense that featured a label of a white female burning incense. Within the smoke of the incense, the face of a man wearing a turban appears to have manifested. The Lucky Heart Company of Memphis used exotic imagery to decorate sales catalogues. A scantily clad white female dressed in exotic clothing can be seen presenting the reader with hand held open, a turban-clad spiritual reader who stands over a crystal ball and images of dice, money, black cats and a wishbone.

Gambling

The magical properties of materials used in hoodoo were frequently used to gain an advantage while gambling and in games of chance. Charms were created by conjurers and frequently sold to aid gamblers. Mass-produced curios provided tools to assist the gambler in the form of oils, powders, candles and incense.

One of the popular tools that became associated with hoodoo curio culture was the dream book. It was claimed that these tomes could interpret dreams and derive supernatural messages to be used in gambling and playing street games, like local lotteries known as "policy." Some of the popular dream books that could be seen in Memphis curio shops included *Aunt Sally's Policy Player's Dream Book*, *Kansas City Kitty Dream Book*, *King Tut Dream Book*, *The Three Witches Dream Dictionary* and *Policy Pete's Dream Book*. A popular book in Chattanooga in the 1940s was *The Lucky Star Dream Book*, written by mysterious "Professor Konje." One of the more prolific titles in Louisville was *The Original Lucky Three Wise Men Dream Book*, from a Professor Zonite.

Memphis has long been known as a haven for rootworkers and magic makers. As early as 1891, spiritual workers in the Delta sought the services of Memphis-based spiritual workers. A conjurer in Jackson, Mississippi, was discovered with a complex form of a charm described this way: "The bag

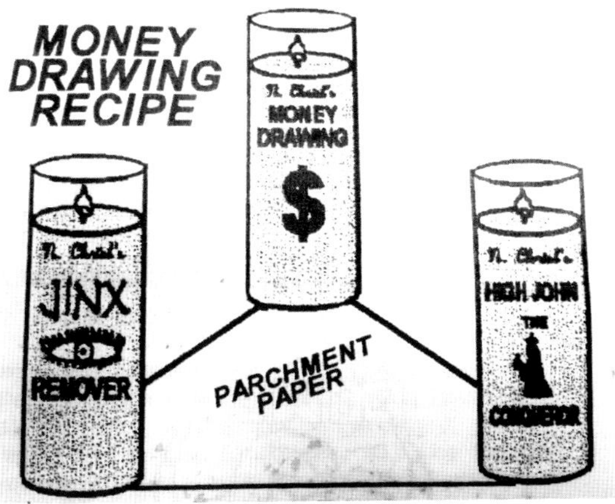

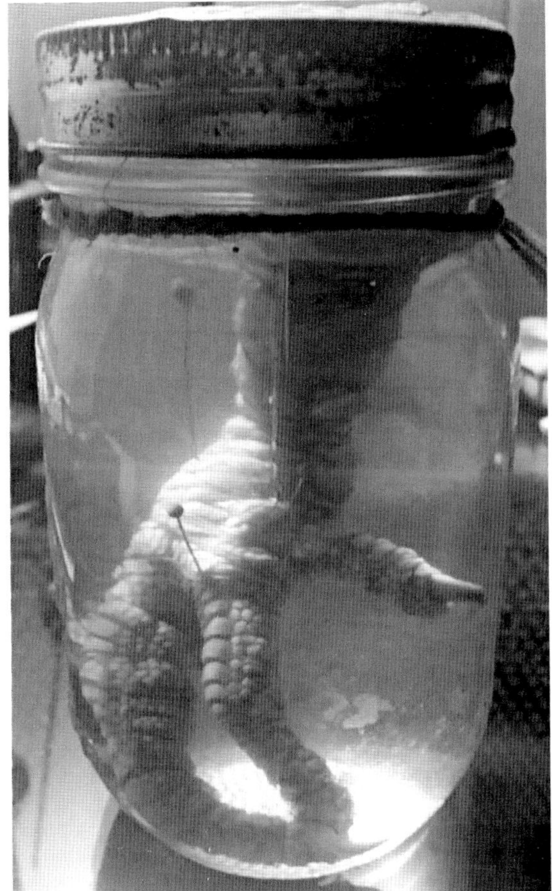

Top: Some Mid-South spiritual workers would order materials from spiritual supply stores that offered written instructions on how to place candles and perform rituals. *Courtesy of author's collection.*

Left: This particular working was used to magically "draw" in money using the chicken's foot wrapped in green thread. *Courtesy of author's collection.*

was made of red flannel and contained a human arm bone, apparently a child's. This bone was wrapped up with snake root, load stone, red pepper and a rabbit foot. In a box he also carried particles of lodestone, blue stone, alum and camphor gum." The conjurer claimed that the bags were purchased from an "old hoodoo woman" in Memphis. The items cost the man fifty cents and were created in order for the man to do well in gambling.

A former employee of A. Schwab on Beale Street tells me that customers would come in and purchase mojo bags to take across the bridge into West Memphis, Arkansas, where they would gamble at the dog and horse track. Likewise, there is evidence that jockeys would use similar curios while racing.

CON MEN

In 1950, in Montgomery, Alabama, a spiritual con man who was discovered to be a veteran of the Spanish-American War began a series of tricks and cons using the fear of hoodoo as a tool. The man would locate a home inhabited by an African American family and knock on the door. When the victim opened the door, the con man would throw an unidentifiable powder onto the victim. Knowing that many families believed in the power of rootwork and conjure materials, the man would then proceed to describe how he could remove the hex he had just placed on them for a specific fee.

HOODOO JUSTICE

While many outsiders to Hoodoo culture showed anger, disgust and confusion when encountering traditional folk practices, some attempted to appropriate elements of the culture for personal gain and power. Following the onslaught of yellow fever epidemics in Memphis in the late 1800s, that city's infrastructure was diminished. The population was dwindling, and the cost to rebuild the city's sewage structure was immense. In 1879, Memphis's board of aldermen voted to relinquish the city's charter. The State of Tennessee granted this and created the tax district of Shelby County. This would create a local government and several county services. A local president was appointed to rule over the new taxing district.

The district's second president was noted by historians to have been one of the most memorable characters in this office. David Park Hadden was president of the district from 1882 to 1889. Hadden also served as a county judge for the district. During his tenure, he was credited as cleaning up much of the city following the devastating epidemics. His personality was also reported to be "larger than life." President Hadden would not only involve himself in local government but also injected himself into the lives of the city's residents. As a judge, Hadden encountered many cases of crimes and assaults tied to individuals cheating while gambling. Hadden created what he called the "Hadden Horn," a horn-shaped device that dice could be rolled out of without the interference of cheating hands or loaded dice.

While in office, President Hadden became known for his eccentric behavior. On one occasion, he placed a rather strange-looking artifact on the desk in his office. A reporter from the *Memphis Appeal* noticed the object and asked the president about its meaning. Hadden smiled and replied, "It is a hoodoo prophet." The reporter described the object as being a mask that had an expression that reminded him of an Egyptian god. The mask was made of horse vertebrae with eyes, nose and mouth drawn on it. The image was painted red and black and adorned with symbols of a sun and moon and what he described as two cabalistic signs. The president told him that the mask had been removed from a "deserted Negro cabin." Hadden told the reporter that he wanted to place the artifact above his head in court to represent a figure of justice. His reasoning was as follows: "As the great majority of persons who are arraigned before the recorder are colored, the effect of the hoodoo item on them will be immense. They already stand in considerable awe of Mr. Hadden but when they find that he is aided and abetted by one of the dreaded idols, they will be still more fearful of him."

As there appears to be no further description of the mask, it does pose some interesting questions. What was that mask? Did it have African or Native American ancestry? Why was it painted red and black? The colors are frequently used to denote the presence of the West African deity Esu, the Yoruba deity Eshu and Papa Legba in Haitian Vodou.

Hoodoo-related justice was believed to have taken many forms. In the mid-1940s, Dainey Deaderick Canfield, known locally as "D.D. Canfield," operated a successful laundry business called the Model Laundry in Nashville. Canfield had been associated with the laundry for over thirty years. Due to a growing number of customers, the workload for employees had skyrocketed. This was good for business but also brought its share of problems. In dealing with such a large amount of clothing to be cleaned, it was expected that a few pieces would occasionally be misplaced. Canfield had just hired a young man and began to notice numerous pieces of clothing disappearing from the business. Canfield ended up paying the customers for their losses, which became a rising expense to the business. He began to keep an eye on the new employee and one day caught the young man wearing a pair of pants that appeared very similar to a pair that had gone missing. Canfield questioned the young boy and called the police. The boy was investigated and arrested.

The next day, the boy's mother hired a well-known local attorney and began to perform spiritual workings to get her son freed. Local media shared information about her quest to free the boy:

> *She purchased one of every known gadget in Nashville that was supposed to bring good luck—High John the Conqueror root, Five Finger Grass, lodestone and half a dozen other items. Then she made two small cloth bags and into each she placed a portion of her purchases. One bag was hung around the neck of her boy who by that time had been released*

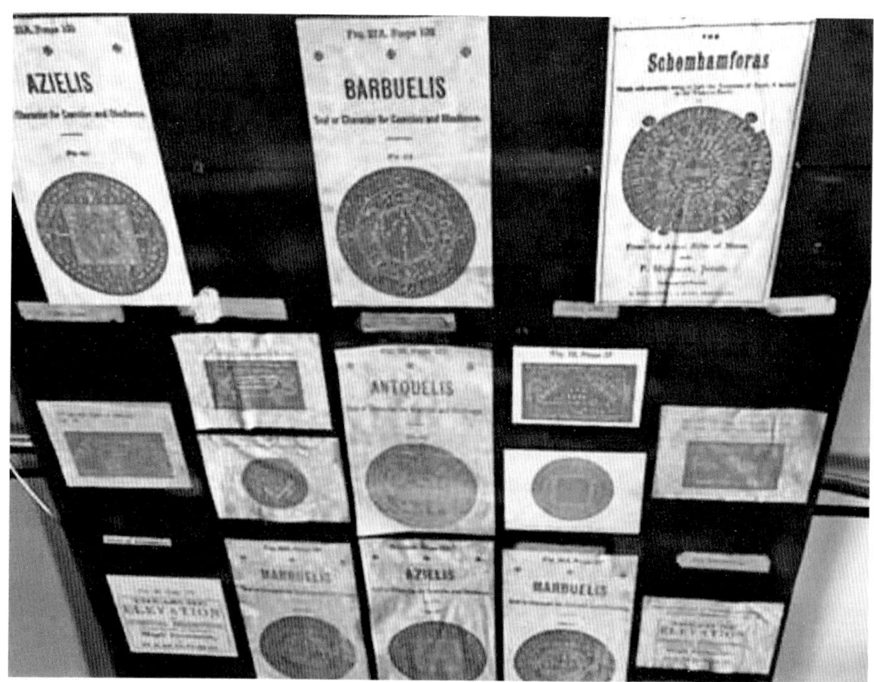

Seals used in summoning spirits from the various Books of Moses. These seals were discovered in storage at A. Schwab on Beale Street in Memphis. *Courtesy of author's collection.*

> *on bond, the other bag went around her own neck. Before the case ever came to a final decision Mr. Canfield died suddenly during a trip to Louisville Kentucky and of course the boy was released for lack of prosecution. He is still free and will remain so, as far as that particular case is concerned.*

Canfield's death was described in his obituary as a result of an unexpected heart attack.

Poisons and Conjure

The belief that African and African American conjurers were responsible for poisoning victims came from two sources. The first was urban legends combined with racist stereotypes perpetrated through the press and early southern communities. The conjurer was frequently depicted as an evil sorcerer who had little to no regard for life and health. The second strand came from some actual cases in which forms of poison had been employed by slaves and some spiritual workers. Poisons are also recognized by several different African communities as a part of life; some traditional spirit workers specialized in the use of poisons. In the African context, some poisons were used in specific magico-religious trials and spiritual tests. Some communities have also used the poisons in self-defense from enemies and as forms of social justice.

One of the high-profile cases that certainly affected how many southerners viewed African traditions and poison occurred in Virginia in 1732. Ambrose Madison, the grandfather of U.S. president James Madison, was killed at the Mount Pleasant Plantation (later known as Montpelier) in Orange, Virginia. The local sheriff and the family believed that his death was caused by poisoning. Three Igbo slaves from Nigeria were charged with the murder. Two of the men were beaten; the third was executed.

The Mid-South would see a number of cases involving African and African American healing and spiritual traditions being associated with intentional and unintentional poisonings. In 1868, two women in Memphis attempted to hire local rootworker Uncle Dub to pour strychnine into the drinking-water cistern of a man believed to have murdered their uncle. The plot failed when Uncle Dub warned the man about the plan to end his life. Both women were arrested by local police.

In 1869, Pastoria, Arkansas police charged a spiritual worker known only as Walker with murder after it was believed he poisoned a woman who came to him seeking treatment. Georgia Grant came to Walker after she discovered that she had an ulcerated throat. Walker provided the woman with an herbal remedy that was supposed to heal her condition. After taking the remedy, Grant soon died. Reports refer to Walker as "the Voodoo." While spiritual healers were not typically recognized as practicing medical professionals by law, Walker was charged with malpractice, as well.

In 1888, a Memphis man attempted to poison his wife based on the supposed advice of a local female conjurer. The conjurer advised Louis Hill to kill a snake and place its venom in his wife's drink seven days away at the seventh hour. Hill killed a water moccasin and attempted to drain its venom. When Hill realized that he couldn't extract the venom, he placed the snake's head into his wife's coffee. The woman began to get violently ill. Hill was eventually arrested for the attempted murder.

In 1907, a spiritual worker was the prime suspect in the poisoning of a black family in Lake Village, Arkansas. Local authorities believed that someone had poured rat poison into the family's well after discovering a bag in the water supply. Investigators later turned their attention to a bag of flour that the family had used in cooking. The poison killed one male family member and left the remaining members very sick.

African American healing traditions and spirituality were frequently spoken of as negative works of sorcery. Practitioners of these healing traditions were commonly called "Voodoos" or "Hoodoos." In cities like Memphis, the term *Congos* was used. Common myths regarding African-inspired practices focused on curses and, in many cases, poisons. A 1950 news article from Montgomery reads, "If a Negro desired to destroy an enemy, he sought the aid of the voodoo, which in many cases would undertake to remove the obnoxious one and the removal was generally accomplished through the medium of poison."

Incidents involving poison and conjure did occur on some occasions. Eight years later, in neighboring Macon, Georgia, items related to conjure were discovered being used by a widow charged with poisoning four people with arsenic. Thirty-three-year-old Anjette Lyles had poisoned two husbands, a mother-in-law and a nine-year-old daughter. Police took interest in her conjure as they discovered packages of good-luck powder, Egyptian love powdered incense and Adam and Eve roots and oil. In addition, a number of recipes were found in the residence, including one featuring a love potion that called for ingredients such as dragon's blood and myrrh. During the trial, it was revealed that Lyles was obsessed with magic and the occult. She had made frequent trips to spiritual advisors and purchased numerous materials, including candles, oils and powders to perform spiritual workings.

The Grand Order of the Black Cat Bone

Sheriff's deputies in Birmingham, Alabama, were bewildered when a man entered the station begging for protection from his wife. "You don't understand, my wife is part of this cult. She turns into animals at night. She has turned into an insect and has kept me awake all night!" As nervous sweat poured from the man's head, the deputies looked at each other. "Want to tell me that again?" said the heavyset deputy, who leaned across a wooden chair in front of him. The gray-haired African American man placed his hand across his heart. "Swear to God sir, my wife has joined this group of some folks from Atlanta. They do some sort of strange stuff that gives them power. They call themselves the Order of the Black Cat Bone." The Grand Order of the Black Cat Bone had come up on the deputy's radar before. In fact, two other people had contacted local police about similar situations in which family members had joined the mysterious group and were alleged to have transformed into various animals and beasts. Further investigation revealed that a gang from Georgia had moved into the area and was putting out information about a "Grand Order of the Black Cat Bone" and offering protection from the group for a "nominal fee."

Snakes in the Stomach

A frequent phenomenon that seemed to appear in the rootworking and conjure culture was the alleged appearance of animals, insects and reptiles in the stomachs of clients who had been crossed. Spiritual healers were believed to have the ability to not only detect these types of workings but also to be able to remove these intestinal invaders. This pathology can be found in a number of traditional healing cultures throughout the world. In the case of southern hoodoo, the origins are most likely African.

Folklorist Newbell Niles Puckett found during his research in the Delta that some communities believed that conjurers would kill reptiles such as snakes and dry them out before grinding them into fine powders. This powder would be slipped into a victim's food and eventually turn into living snakes inside the body. Puckett mentions that some variations of this type of work include the use of powdered snake fangs or fat. These can also be placed through cracks in the victim's ceiling or inside his shoes. Snake blood can also be added to milk, whereby the victim will ingest the powder. It is also believed that a horsehair placed in water will eventually turn into a snake. Horsehair was also placed in milk to be ingested by the victim. Anvil dust placed in a victim's food will eventually cause snakes to grow inside of him.

Cultural informants shared with Puckett that people with reptiles in their stomachs displayed certain types of symptoms. Some conjurers claimed that the reptile would be visible in the throat of the victim. Nervous twitches were viewed as symptoms of reptile invasion. The conjured would begin to have a large appetite then eventually would stop eating foods that they typically ate. They may also begin making strange animal noises. In some cases, mosquitos were believed to have flown out of a conjured victim's head.

Remedies to remove snakes and insects from the conjured included teas made from snakeroot and silk-root. Tinctures made from snakeroot and whiskey were also used to combat these types of workings.

As early as 1869, there is a record of these types of instances in the Mid-South. In Natchez, Mississippi, spiritual healer Emily Gibson advertised her ability to remove animals such as lizards, snakes, frogs and insects from the inside of those stricken with conjure. Gibson was alleged to have removed several things from inside patients in the African American and white communities. Gibson, however, wound up in trouble with the law when she was taken to court for obtaining money under false pretenses. She was acquitted of the charges and soon took her work some two hours away to Greenville, Mississippi.

Nineteen years later, in Birmingham, Alabama, the phenomenon resurfaced, this time inside of animals. Four black men were murdered after it was believed they were responsible for the deaths of two horses belonging to a Sarah Moore of Birmingham. Moore told authorities that she believed her horses had been "voodooed." She obtained a doctor to perform an autopsy on the animals. The doctor discovered a small snake in one of the horses' stomachs and a lizard in the other's. Tragically, the "mystical death" of the horses took prominence over the importance of the four men who had been murdered, as local papers explained, "In this section the killing of the negro is regarded as a matter of little importance so no very determined effort has been made to solve the mystery of these four crimes." Once again, the fear of African culture took priority over the value placed on human lives.

Were these staged incidents? Were they real? Back in 1849, German scientist Arnold Berthold conducted a study using insects and reptiles that had been removed from the inside or vomited out of human bodies. Each one of the specimens contained partially digested insects, which led Dr. Berthold to conclude that many of these creatures had been deliberately swallowed. Were Mid-South healers and conjurers using tricks to create these occurrences?

Remnants of Africa

Cultural traditions from Africa can be found in the physical landscape of the Mid-South. Various materials representing spiritual forces and metaphysical artifacts appear mundane to those who do not comprehend their uses. Early southerners found some of these items that were born in Mother Africa, and people throughout the Mid-South today can still find them.

Throughout the Mid-South, there are three distinct African traditions that can still be seen today. The use of "yard decorations," "grave decorations" and "bottle trees" are all manifestations of African cultural practices.

Yard decorations may appear to be simplistic, unorganized landscaping that makes use of statues, glass, metals and wood. However mundane this may appear, a symbolic message and technique are being communicated by its owner. Materials may include plates nailed to trees and placed on planted wooden sticks. Various wheels, blades and tires may be placed in a yard. In the book *No Space Hidden: The Spirit of African-American Yard Work* by Grey Gundaker and Judith McWillie, these items are described as having spiritual qualities. "Circular motion manifested in rotating fan blades, automobile wheel rims, clock faces, white washed tires and other round or spherical objects recalls the rising and setting of the sun."

Some yards contain statues and figures used to represent various spiritual personalities. Dogs, lambs, lions, children, angels, saints and Native

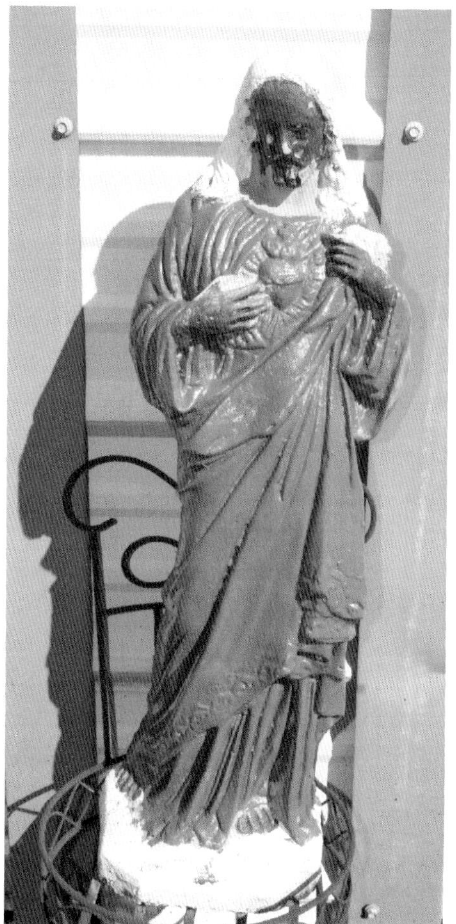

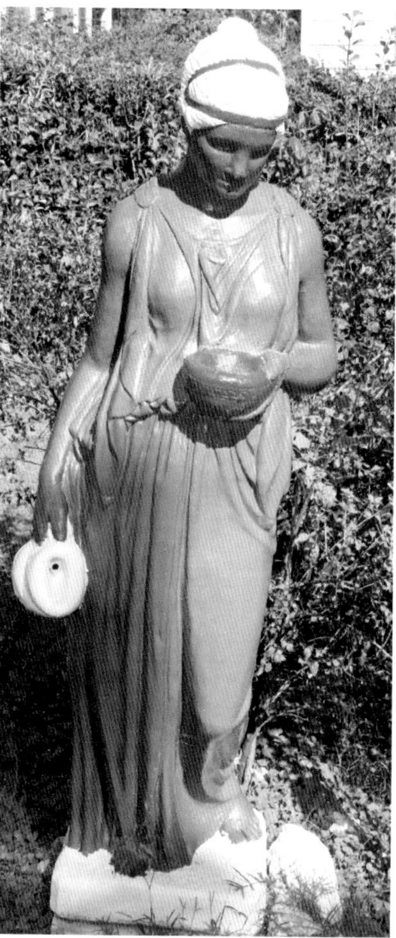

Left: There are three distinct African traditions that can be seen in the Mid-South, including bottle trees, grave decorations and yard decorations. Materials have symbolic meaning and can convey messages such as protection, divinity and the movement of the sun. *Courtesy of author's collection.*

Right: African culture in the Mid-South is frequently, as one writer states, "Hidden in plain sight." *Courtesy of author's collection.*

American images may be placed at various thresholds in yards. These serve as watchers or guardians of the home. Gundaker and McWillie speak of these objects as messengers of judgement and authority.

The practice of decorating grave sites is a tradition that can be traced back to West Africa. Materials such as shells, white rocks, clocks, mirrors, telephones and toys can be found on some grave sites in the Mid-South. Some materials are placed there, as they were considered the last object touched by the deceased. Coins may be placed at some grave sites to guide the dead away from the land of the living. Ceramic pitchers filled with water reflect African beliefs regarding water separating the land of the living from that of the dead. The presence of water at the site is believed to help assist the dead in their transition between worlds. Water is an important element in African traditions and has strong spiritual meaning in most African religious traditions. As Kongo religious traditions had a strong influence on healing and spiritual cultures of the Mid-South, it is no surprise that spiritual concepts concerning water would be found in the region. To the Bakongo people, water represents Kalunga, the body of water that separates the land of the living and the land of the dead.

One of the most iconic images of the rural Mid-South is the bottle tree. The bottle tree is a living or dead tree with glass bottles placed on its branches or hanging from them by string. In some bottle trees, materials such as tinfoil, metallic reflective materials and even bones are placed on branches. In many cases, the bottles are blue in color. The use of blue in some trees is reflective of the concept known as "haint blue." This is the colloquial term to describe a shade of blue frequently used in the South that is believed to keep away negative forces. The concept is thought to have come from the Gullah people of Georgia and South Carolina.

The bottle tree itself comes from the Kongo region of Africa. The Bakongo people would hang pieces of reflective materials such as glass, bottles and gourds to protect homes and crops from spirits. Kym S. Rice and Martha B. Katz write in *World of a Slave*: "The evil spirits would be attracted to the dancing sunlight passing through the bottles and upon entering they would be trapped and prevented from harming the household or its possessions and products. Thieves would see these trees and would be afraid to enter, believing that they would be cursed. Accounts are recorded of enslaved African Americans using similar methods in their garden to prevent stealing and to ensure a bountiful harvest."

The interior of bottles found in bottle tress may be filled with stones, sand, water or graveyard dirt. The bottles' lips may be covered in grease. These materials are believed to "draw" the spirit inside the bottle.

DEALING WITH THE DEAD

Gravediggers bury bodies with the head of the body facing west. It is a tradition in some African American homes in the Mid-South to turn mirrors and photographs around when someone in the home has died. There is a belief that the image of the dead can tarnish mirrors and that it is bad luck for the image to be reflected in a mirror. According to Puckett: "On the Gold Coast of Africa it is a common practice to bring dirt from a man's burial place if he died far away from home or better to bring a piece of his clothes. Thus the returning spirit will find he has not been neglected by his family, and will therefore be disinclined to trouble them with sickness and misfortune."

In 1891, a Mississippi man was arrested for carrying a concealed weapon. When police searched him, they discovered he was also carrying a bag full of materials used in conjure. The red flannel bag contained a child's arm bone. The bone was wrapped with snake root, lodestone, red pepper and a rabbit's foot. He also was carrying a small box that contained lodestone, bluestone, alum and camphor gum. The man claimed that he had purchased the items from a woman he described as an "old hoodoo woman" from Memphis.

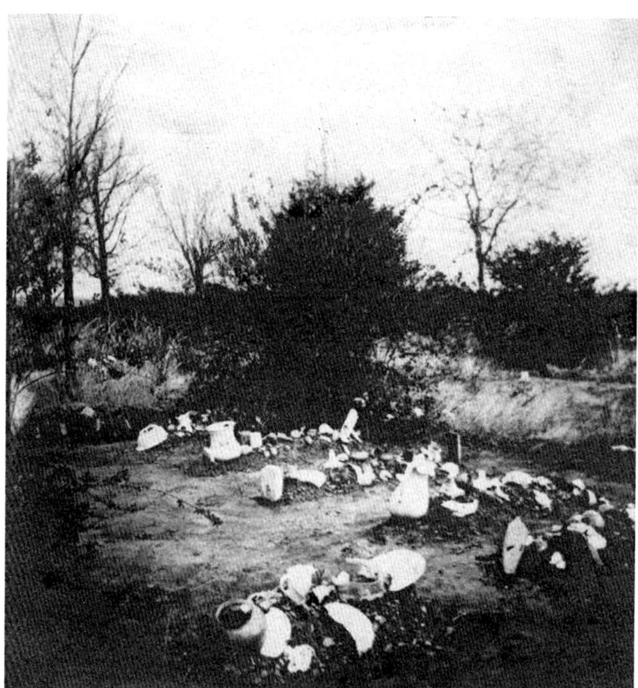

The African-based tradition of decorating grave sites and leaving artifacts belonging to the departed can be seen in some Mid-South cemeteries. *Courtesy of Alabama Department of Archives.*

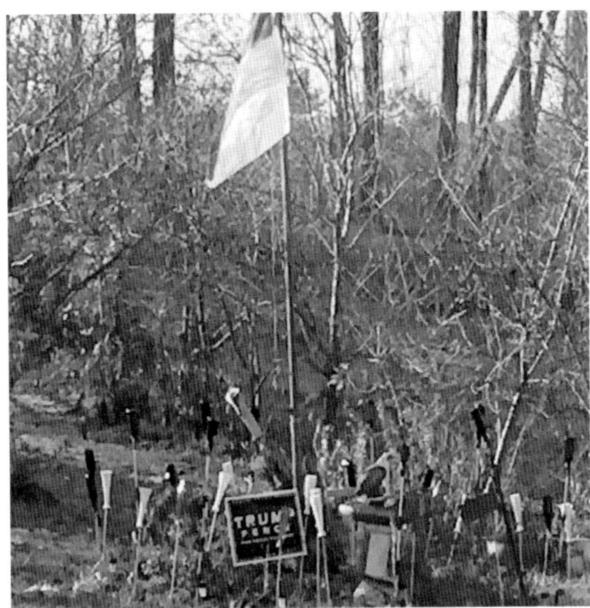

The use of bottle trees in the Mid-South traces its origin back to African spiritual techniques. The bottles are spirit traps that draw spirits in and protect the property from being affected. This particular set of bottle trees is located in Northeast Mississippi. *Courtesy of author's collection.*

As items related to the dead were used throughout Mid-South conjure culture, some artifacts ranged from the mundane to the bizarre. In 1905, local authorities in Louisville made a grim discovery when it was found that the body of a deceased infant was being used as a magical charm. The charm was discovered when Kentucky resident Sallie Anderson told a judge that her roommate, Carrie Anderson, had stolen the nine-week-old baby that Sallie had placed in a jar of alcohol. Anderson claimed that her husband, who worked at a local hospital, had gotten the child's corpse and brought it home. Anderson stated to the court, "I called it my hoodoo baby and as long as it stayed on my mantlepiece [*sic*], I had good luck." The judge asked Anderson about the luck that the charm had allegedly produced. Anderson replied, "I wus doubled up wid rheumatism till de hoodoo baby come, an now I's as agile as a colt. It wont last though, lessen I get dat baby back. De minute I found it missin dis mornin I felt a rheumatic pain shoot through my elbow and I knowed what it meant." Sallie then proceeded to take out a warrant against Carrie Anderson for taking the charm.

In 1935, an Alabama conjurer was shot and killed by police. The fifty-eight-year-old man, Lige Gray, had been the talk of the community, as the local sheriff's department discovered several cow and horse heads placed on the fence around his home. Gray had been rumored to be disturbing graves in order to contact spirits of the deceased. A group of men began

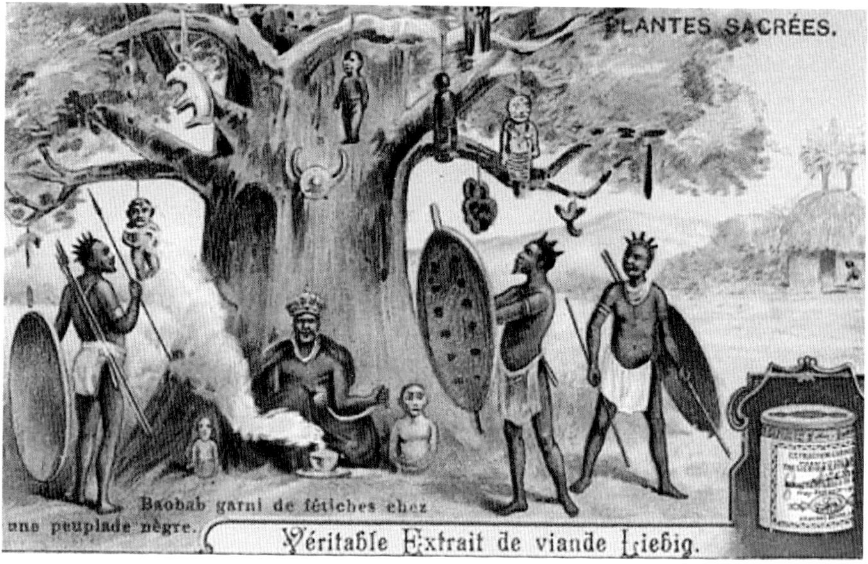

Artist's depiction of "Fetish" trees in Africa. Ritual specialists would place various sacred artifacts in the trees for protection. This same technique can be seen among bottle trees and some decorated trees in the Mid-South. *Public domain.*

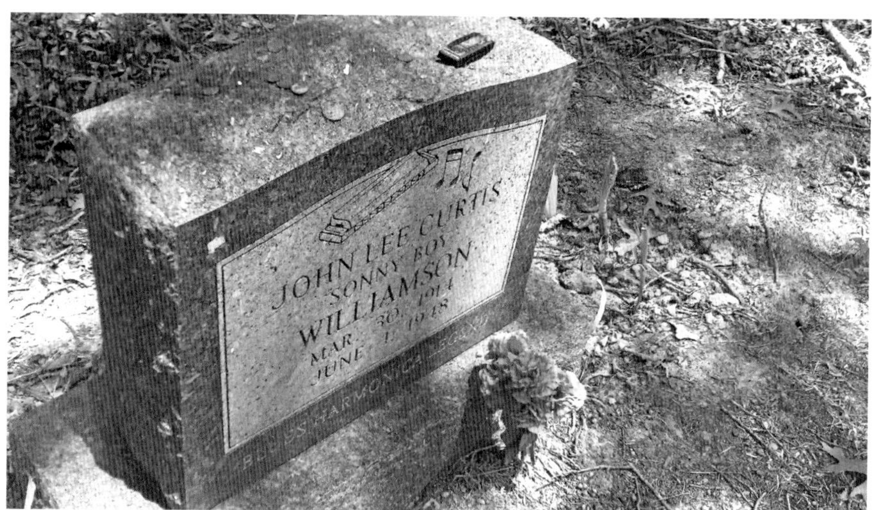

Grave site of blues legend Sonny Boy Williamson in West Tennessee. Coins are frequently left on tombstones in the Mid-South to purchase graveyard dirt and favors from the dead. *Courtesy of author's collection.*

to patrol the local cemetery at night to keep away trespassers. The men discovered Gray disturbing a grave site and contacted the sheriff. When deputies arrived, there was a standoff with Gray. He was ordered to put down the shovel he was using to dig into a grave. The report says that Gray attacked the men with the shovel and was shot and killed. The deputies discovered a belt around the conjurer containing small slits that were filled with human bones.

Madame Hightower

The year was 1925, and thousands of African American women throughout the South had found a specialized line of cosmetics that catered strictly to the African American community. Golden Brown Chemical Company of Memphis, Tennessee, was the premier manufacturer of such great beauty products as Golden Brown Hair Dressing, Flowers of Liberia Perfume, Golden Brown Talc Powder and dozens of other products. Golden Brown advertisements were not only prominent in the South but were also soon placed in many of the nation's black newspapers, from the *Chicago Defender* to the *Philadelphia Tribune*. The company's ads promoted alternative products for the African American community. Ads promised that Golden Brown products had helped one woman clear her complexion so much that it helped her win the most wonderful husband in the world. And why wouldn't they?

You see, Golden Brown cosmetics was started by an African American woman named Madame Mamie Hightower. Madame Hightower was an exemplary example of small-town woman makes it big. She started out with very little but rose to run a multimillion-dollar company, even in the face of racism in the South. Hightower's image was depicted in many of the company's ads and promotional works. Her graceful and lovely silhouette demonstrated to her customers the proof that her products were quite sufficient in bringing out the beauty in African Americans.

Golden Brown began to build quite a reputation as a friend to the black community. In 1925, the company sponsored a national Golden Brown Beauty Contest, inviting women of every race to participate for fantastic grand prizes, including five free trips to Atlantic City and forty-eight genuine diamond rings for runners-up. The grand-prize winner of the contest received a brand-new Hudson automobile. Madame Hightower was truly pushing for black women in America to stand proud and display their beauty. She is quoted in an ad as saying, "I will not be content until I find the most beautiful girl of our group in America."

Soon, Golden Brown cosmetics were becoming popular outside of the South, with new customer bases in areas like Chicago and New York. The firm's cosmetics were taking off, and Madame Hightower continued to speak to her fans through her ads and even in an advice column company ran in many newspapers. The good madame built racial pride as she encouraged women, "You are judged by your personal appearance, the race is judged by you." It seemed that she truly wanted women to have a sense of pride and accomplishment. This despite the fact that many of the company's ads featured African American women turning light-skinned and European-looking as they used the company's products.

Golden Brown really seemed to be in touch with the community, as Madame Hightower opened a beauty salon on Beale Street in Memphis. Operating out of the "boulevard for black America," as it was once known, Golden Brown became a trusted name in African American products. The company began to proclaim about Beale, "Handy made it famous with his blues, Madame Hightower immortalizes it with her incomparable beauty preparations." Ads came to feature an array of beautiful women, known as the "Famous Bobbed-Hair Beauties." The ladies were commonly featured as being customers of Golden Brown cosmetics. Readers could order color photographs of the ladies who featured in the musical *Shuffle Along*, which played first in Harlem and then in Manhattan.

In 1926, a trusted secret of the company came out. Madame Hightower released an ad in which she spoke about a gift her Aunt Nancy had given her that, she believed, brought her luck and, ultimately, financial success. Hightower's aunt gave her a magical object, described as a "Ma-Jo Luck Bag," that was soon credited with bringing about the formation and success of the Golden Brown Chemical Company. Even better was the fact that Madame Hightower was offering these bags to her customers as a way of continuing the preservation of African American culture in the South. The bag was deemed so authentic that one ad described it as an "Algerian" Ma-Jo Bag. This description was a nod to the reputation of Algiers, Louisiana, which had become legendary as a place to find hoodoo-related objects and services.

According to its ads, Golden Brown's cosmetics were now being offered in over twelve thousand drugstores throughout the United States. Pharmacies in white communities were carrying a line of products now being used by

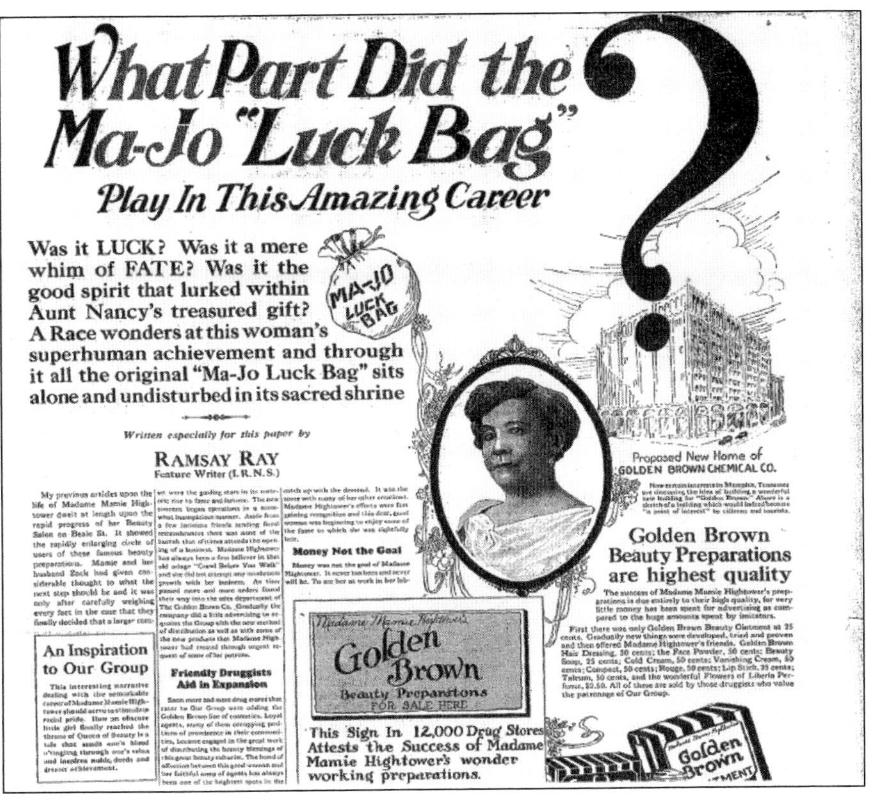

DIED IN TENNESSEE

Above: The mysterious Madame Hightower offered a "Ma-Jo" luck bag for her customers that was believed to be her source of financial success. The bag was alleged to have come from Algiers, Louisiana, a legendary hot spot for hoodoo practitioners. *Courtesy of* Pittsburgh Courier.

Left: The powerful Madame Hightower was discovered to be a sales gimmick created by the owners of Golden Brown Chemical Company in Memphis. *Courtesy of author's collection.*

black and white customers. Madame Mamie Hightower's dream was coming to fruition. The world would know her products.

In March 1929, a single piece of paper would change this forever. A Chicago-based African American druggist who operated the Douglass Pharmacy opened his mail to find a formal letter from the Golden Brown Chemical Company of Memphis. The letter, obviously meant for white pharmacists and cosmetic shop owners, described the addition of the lucky "Ma-Jo Bag" now being offered by the company. The letter proclaimed, "The average darky will be very glad indeed to get one of these dyed-in-the-red Luck Bags."

The letter was sent to the attention of local newspapers and then, nationally, to black-owned newspapers. Many in the black community wondered, "How could Madame Hightower allow this?" Sadly, she couldn't.

Madame Mamie Hightower did not exist. Not as a CEO of a company, not as a woman who received a magic luck bag that changed her life and, sadly, not as a rags-to-riches role model. Mamie Hightower was the wife of Zachary Hightower, a janitor and porter for Golden Brown Chemical. The company was set up as a "dummy company" by the white-owned Hessig-Ellis wholesale drug company and employed thirty-five African American employees. In an attempt to cash in on the success of other African American cosmetic companies, Golden Brown began to feature ads recruiting African Americans as sale agents. In October 1947, the company was charged with misrepresentation in connection with the promise of "free goods" for sales agents. Another incident targeting the black community…

Even in Mamie Hightower's death announcement in October 1927, the Madame Hightower ruse was still being promoted. Deemed an "internationally known beauty culturist and philanthropist," Hightower was credited as being the "originator of the famous Golden Brown Beauty Preparations."

The story of Madame Hightower and the Golden Brown Chemical Company is, tragically, one of many incidents in Memphis hoodoo history involving racism and the exploitation of the African American community. Hoodoo in Memphis was first feared, then suppressed, then exploited. But through it all, the practices and traditions rooted in African soil survived and flourished in the Mid-South.

Pharmacies

Materials used in the practice of rootwork and conjure appeared in many pharmacies throughout the Mid-South. Establishments such as Hub City Pharmacy in Hattiesburg, Mississippi, sold traditional western medicines but also featured a number of curious used in the practice of African American folk healing. The shop carried oils, powders, incense and candles. Oils such as money drawing and fast luck could be purchased from the pharmacy shelves. Sprays such as Doctor Pryor's Spiritual House Blessing, Gambler's Lucky-Play Deodorant Spray and 9 Indian Herb Jinx Removing Offering Spray were frequently purchased by customers. Adam and Eve Candles, Dragon's Blood, Winning Number Powdered Incense and Lucky Number Powdered Incense were sure to bring health, healing and luck to the fortunate customer. A brochure from LaClarix, "The Mystic Challenge," used to be carried in the shop and advised customers on how to use many of the shop's products. "Read the Bible to help court cases. Psalm 142. Anoint yourself with King Solomon High John Oil with Root. Anoint the root with oil and carry it with you. Was with High John the Conqueror Soap and add King Solomon Bath Pellets to your bath before your court case."

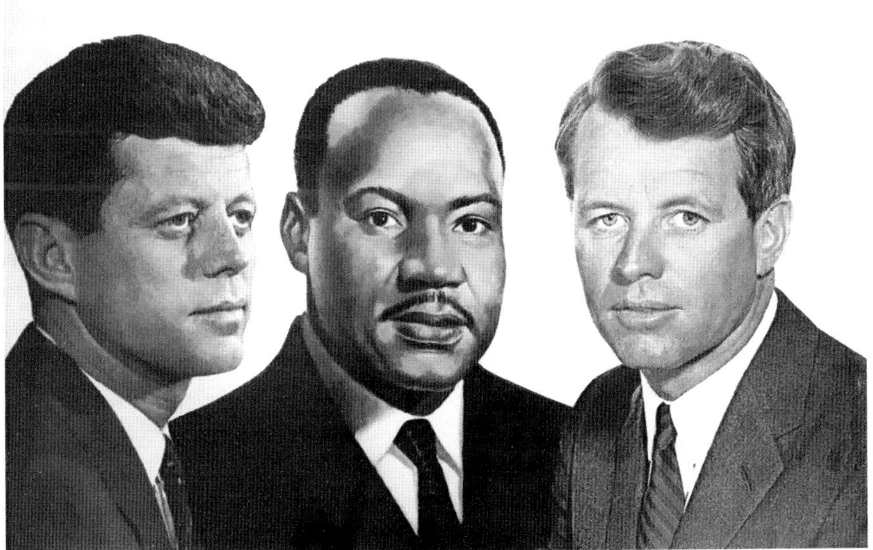

Spiritual shops that accommodated both African Americans and Caucasians would place an image of Dr. Martin Luther King Jr., John F. Kennedy and Robert Kennedy as a sign that all were welcome. *Courtesy of author's collection.*

Hardy Street Pharmacy on Hardy Street in Hattiesburg carried a number of spiritual supplies. Owner Fred A. Waits opened the store in 1955 and offered local Mississippians medicines, electronics and cosmetics. Waits had inherited the shop from a former owner, who had offered a number of spiritual products to customers. Waits began getting calls and inquiries from former customers seeking hoodoo-related materials. Waits began to stock curios and herbs, including candles, floor washes, oils and powders. Waits passed away in 2004.

Harmon's Drugstore on Farish Street in Jackson, Mississippi, became known as a place where one could purchase materials for charms, roots and herbs, as well as several assorted curios. Pharmacist George Harmon told the *Clarion-Ledger* that he began selling hoodoo-related products because a friend suggested he could make money on the idea. His friend, a druggist in New Orleans, had great success selling hoodoo-related curios, even offering to give Doc Harmon some products to see if customers would buy them. Harmon discovered that customers loved the curios and that he couldn't keep them in stock, they were selling so fast. Harmon was nicknamed by local media as a "voodoo pharmacist," although he never claimed to be. He told a reporter that the curios made up half of his business but that he never advised customers on how to use any of the materials. The pharmacy carried various oils, powders and candles, along with loose-bundled herbs like John the Conqueror and materials like lodestone. Doc Harmon passed away at the age of eighty-five in June 2012. His reputation for helping the community was described in his obituary: "His desire to heal people was a primary reason for choosing to become a pharmacist and this he did, whether through prescription or advice. Doc was a true community servant who never abandoned Farish Street."

Sonny Boy Products on Third Avenue in Birmingham, Alabama, is a legendary name in hoodoo-related curio products. Sonny Boy still operates as a manufacturer and shop for rootworking and conjure-related goods. Following the tradition of many historical pharmacies and curio shops in the Mid-South, A. Schwab on Beale Street in Memphis once carried Sonny Boy items, as did many other regional shops. Sonny Boy Products is located in a discreet building with little signage indicating its location. Originally located in Miami, Florida, Sonny Boy Products became famous for its candles, incense, oils and powders used by spiritual workers throughout the South. Sonny Boy produced a pamphlet called "The Original Sonny Boy Products Alleged Guide to Success and Power!" The pamphlet was available in many stores throughout the Mid-South that carried rootwork

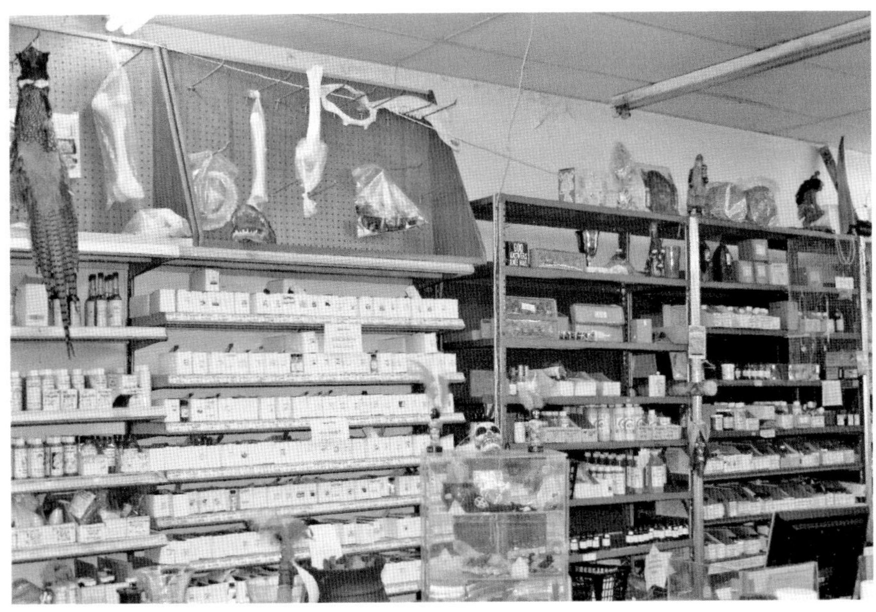

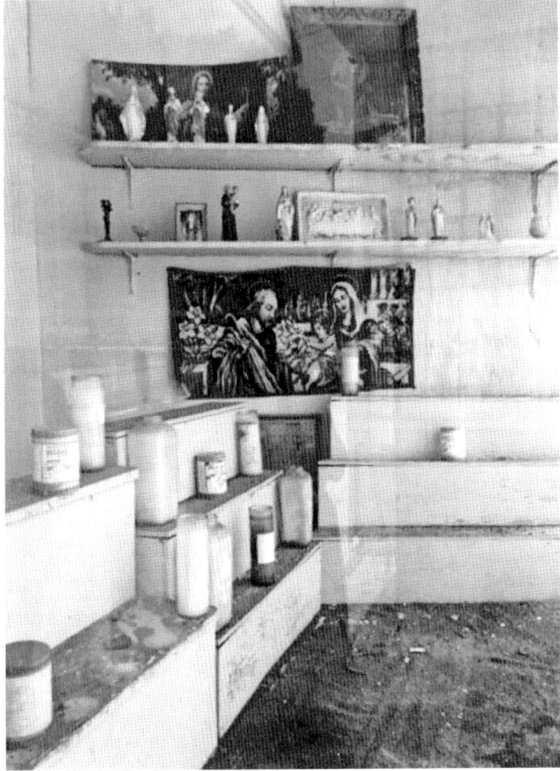

Above: Mid-South spiritual supply stores like Miller's Rexall in Georgia have a long history of providing customers with the accouterments used in rootwork and conjure. *Courtesy of author's collection.*

Left: Some Mid-South shops that carry rootworking materials are discreet in their appearance and decoration. Customers typically find out about their location via word of mouth. *Courtesy of author's collection.*

and conjure supplies. The pamphlet states, "The statements made are not to be accepted as facts but only to tell you of the strange things people do and believe. We make no claims to these saying being of help to anyone." (This was a standard disclaimer that many producers of curios included with their products to avoid issues related to liability.) The pamphlet suggested that by burning three boxes of the company's Love Drawing Power Incense three times a week for three weeks, customers could bring love into their life. Financial blessings were available to those who used the product known as Glory Water and a container of Indian Spray. In Carolyn Morrow Long's *Spiritual Merchants: Religion, Magic and Commerce*, the owner of a pharmacy in Charleston, South Carolina, is quoted as saying that Sonny Boy Products are considered by most black southerners to have the most potency.

Curio Shop was located on Charlotte Avenue in Nashville, Tennessee. In 1949, an African American businessman by the name of Saml A. Tisdale opened a shop catering to the spiritual needs of the local rootworking community. Tisdale had encountered several health problems in his life and was inspired to open a shop dealing in health and spiritual wellness. He received financial assistance to open the store from the rehabilitation division of the Tennessee Department of Welfare. Tisdale's store provided several staples of hoodoo activity, including many of the products

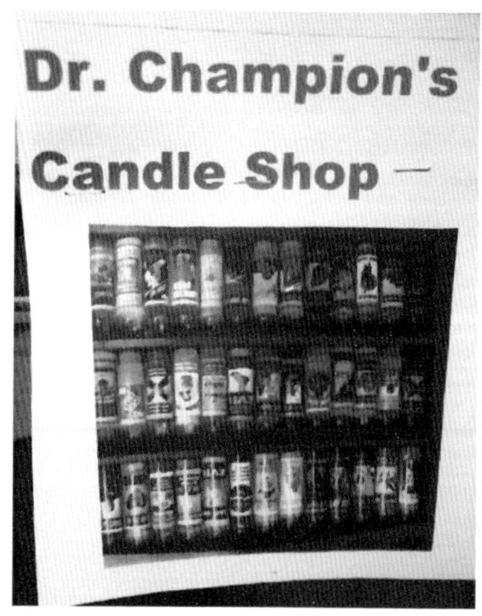

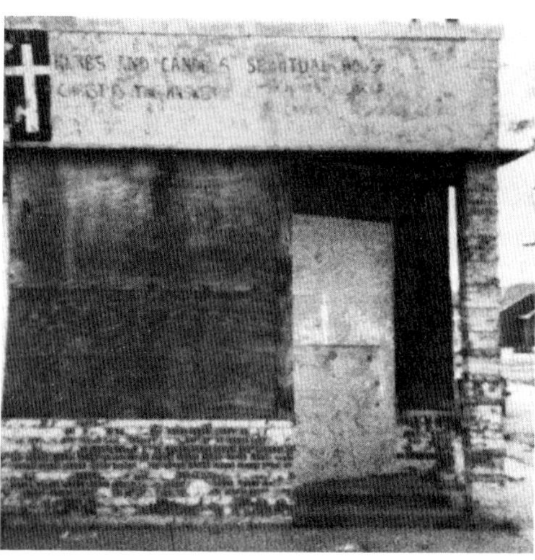

Left: Some pharmacies in the Mid-South still carry hoodoo-related curios. Champion's Pharmacy in Memphis still maintains a section of candles, powders, roots and oils. *Courtesy of author's collection.*

Right: Abandoned spiritual supply store in Jackson, Mississippi. The sign reads "Herbs and Candals Spiritual House, Jesus Is the Answer." *Courtesy of author's collection.*

manufactured by Memphis-based Curio Products Company. Signs inside Tisdale's store advertised "Dragon's Blood Powder," "Success Oil" and "Genuine Lodestone." Shelves were stocked with Lucky Dice Oil, Come to Me Powder, Keep Away Oil and Follow Me Boys Powder.

Burke's Drug Store was located in Montgomery, Alabama, on North Court and Monroe Streets and, later, on South Perry Street. The store offered a number of traditional curious, from candles to powders, for more than one hundred years. The shop started with a small section of curios, but when demand increased, the inventory came to take up half of the store. Employees were known for making mojo bags based on the customer's needs. The store originally had a pharmacist but eventually stopped operating as a pharmacy and turned the pharmacist's counter into a seed cabinet, where customers could purchase plant seeds.

6

AS THE ROOT GROWS

I use the power of prayer, with a few herbs and ingredients to cure my patients.
—Eugene Carey, Memphis healer

The historical lineage of rootwork and conjure in the Mid-South is fascinating. The creation and expansion of various specialists and shops where materials are available for use in hoodoo is ever-changing. The social network that connected individuals, organizations and businesses gave birth to several others. A spiritual healer might know where to direct a client to someone who may be proficient in laying tricks on others. A pharmacy or spiritual supply shop may be on a first-name basis with local healers and spiritual workers whom they can recommend to clients. This same network can give birth to apprentices and businesses.

Take a look at the example of network connections among spiritual doctors, conjurers and businesses in Memphis and Mississippi. The store known as A. Schwab provided spiritual supplies to Arkansas's Madam Glover. Madam Glover worked alongside Dr. Charles Champion in Arkansas. Dr. Champion came to Memphis and opened Champion's Pharmacy. He inherited his pill-cutting machine from the original owner of the hoodoo curio pharmacy Miller's Rexall in Atlanta, Georgia, which sells roots and curios. Dr. Champion sells curios in his pharmacy and became associated with Mississippi pharmacist George Harmon. Harmon opened Harmon Drug in Mississippi and began to also sell roots and curios. The root continues to grow.

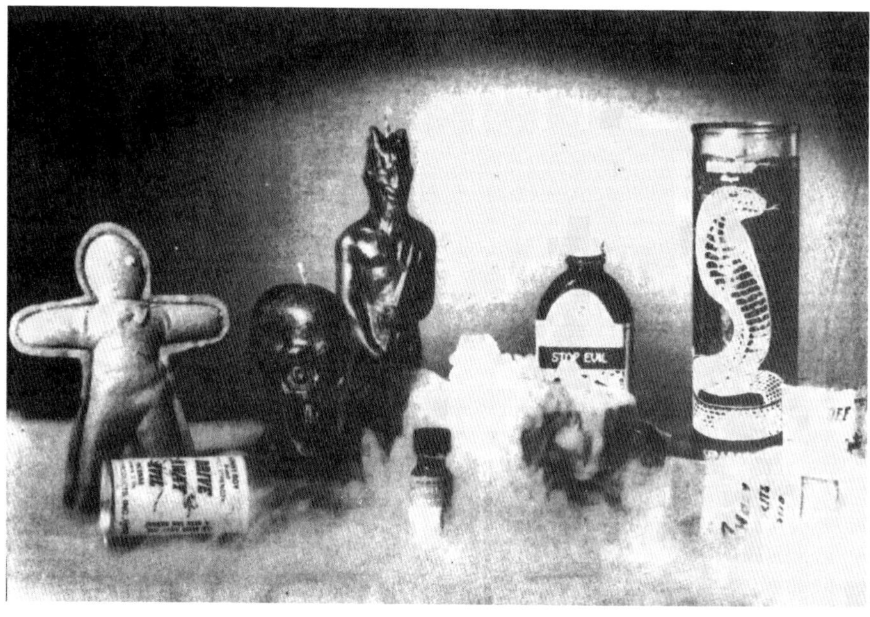

Above: Candles, powders and oils available at one Mississippi spiritual supply store. *Courtesy of* Alabama Journal.

Right: Spiritual healers and rootworkers in the Mid-South frequently toured various states, offering spiritual services to clients in hotel rooms and local shops. *Courtesy of* Alabama Journal.

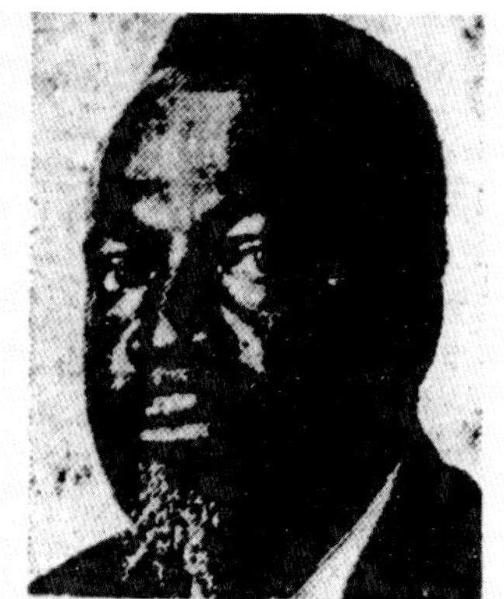

See Rev. Swain & Sister Mary of Atlanta, Ga.
Devine healers and spiritual advisors.
No Problems or sickness is to hard for God. Rev. Swain & Sister Mary will help you.
Phone 269-9486
2359 Roosevelt Street
Montgomery, Alabama
NOTICE: Sister Mary will also come to your home.

CAN YOU KEEP A SECRET? ACTION SPEAKS LOUDER THAN WORDS!!!!!

THE WORLD'S MOST GIFTED PROPHET JESSE, THE KING OF THE BLESSINGS AND THE MASTER OF ALL CASES.
ONE DAY ONE WAY BLESSING, GUARANTEED TO WIN OR HE'LL PAY FOR YOUR LOSS.
CASES SOLVED IN 36 HOURS. DOCTOR BUZZARD'S ONE AND ONLY SON. MANY HAVE TRIED TO IMITATE HIM BUT NONE HAVE DUPLICATED HIM

August 1-2 Chattanooga Tenn 919 Magnolia Call Mrs. Ruth Kenniebrew for Directions 1 (615) 267-3579.
August 8-9 Ft. Pierce Fla. Waterfront Hotel Avenue T 1 (305) 461-4482

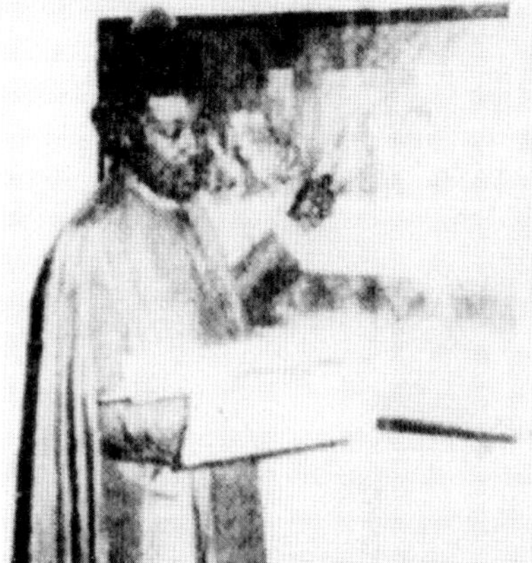

PROPHET JESSE'S VISION IS TO BUILD A CITY FOR GOD AND ALL GOD'S CHILDREN

I HAVE A SURE HIT FOR YOU WHEREVER YOU MAY BE

I HAVE OPEN MY HOTEL FOR YOU THAT WANT TO COME TO MIAMI

Prophet Jesse has seen the hand writing on the Wall God gave Prophet Jesse, the number just like he gave it to John

PROPHET JESSE, DOCTOR BUZZARD'S SON OF BUFORD, SOUTH CAROLINA IS IN MIAMI, FLORIDA CALL RIGHT NOW! ACTION LINE OPEN 24 HOURS MASTER OF ALL CASES

Don't let bad luck hold you back See me today and start being lucky Sure Hits Daily!!!

1. **Guaranteed to get that man back**
2. **Guaranteed to make you win at the track**
3. **Guaranteed to get peace in your home**
4. **Guaranteed to remove Bad Luck**
5. **Guaranteed to get that woman back**
6. **Guaranteed good health**
7. **Guaranteed to win that case in court**
8. **Guaranteed case work**

CAN BE SEEN AT
QUEEN ELIZABETH'S
RELIGIOUS STUDIO
4401 N.W. 7th AVENUE MIAMI, FLORIDA

PHONE 754-1338
4401 N.W. 7th Avenue
THE ACTION LINE IS
OPEN 24 HOURS DAILY
FOR YOU THAT CANNOT COME TO MIAMI, FLA.
CALL AREA CODE (305)754-1338

NO MAIL PLEASE

COME OR CALL

One of the most famous spiritual doctors in hoodoo history was Carolina conjurer Stephany Robinson (aka "Doctor Buzzard"). Many spiritual workers who visited the Mid-South claimed to be Doctor Buzzard or a descendant of the legendary root man. *Courtesy of* Pittsburgh Courier.

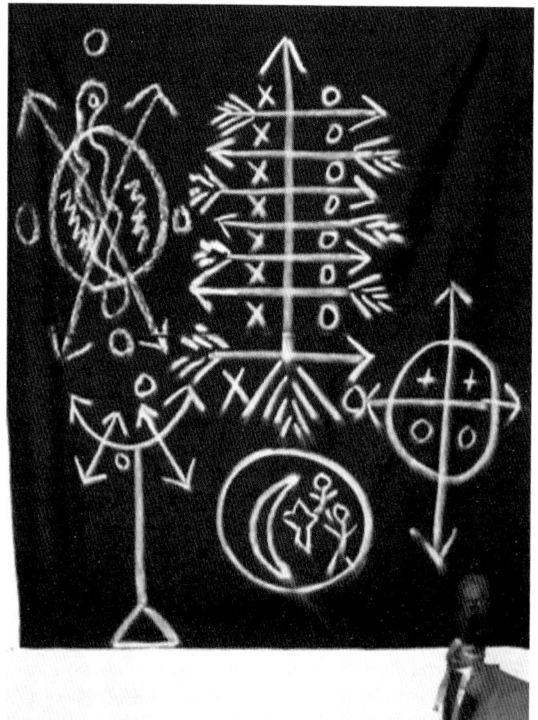

Left: Sacred drawing known as "firma" located in a Mid-South business. The owner of the business maintained a shrine to the spirits of the Bakongo people in the religious practices of Las Reglas de Kongo. Ironically, it is from the Bantu people of the Kongo that the Mid-South attained the concept of the "mojo bag." *Courtesy of author's collection.*

Below: The roots of African spirituality continue in the Mid-South. This shrine to the Yoruba ocean goddess Yemaya is maintained by a priestess of the religion of Regla de Ocha, commonly known as "Santeria." *Courtesy of author's collection.*

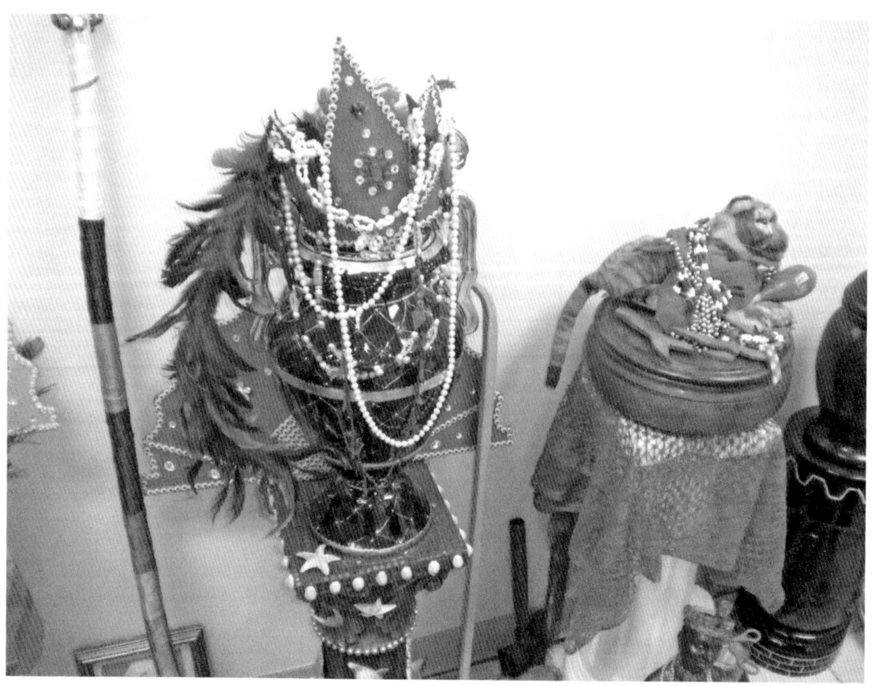

There is an old argument among practitioners that the hoodoo culture subsided with the advent of commercially made curio products and mail-order roots. In the age of the Internet, we now have online courses in rootwork and conjure, plus an array of online shops selling herbs, roots and traditional materials. Materials formerly sold and used secretly are now in the grasp of the general public.

Some shops in the Mid-South maintain ties to traditional healers, but unfortunately, many elders are passing away. Some shops in the Mid-South operated by relatives of healers use recipes and practices handed down by family members. Then there are those healers and conjurers who operate out of their homes and in the back of shops known only to the local community.

The root of African traditional healing and spirituality still maintains a presence in the Mid-South. Many African traditional religions have made the region their home and keep that pulse of Africa alive. Mid-South communities have become the home to a number of temples and practitioners of numerous faiths, including Regla de Ocha (Santeria), Ifa, Las Reglas de Kongo and Vodou. A number of devotees, priests and priestesses maintain traditional African practices throughout the South. Like rootwork and conjure, these cultures keep the root alive.

BIBLIOGRAPHY

Abbeville (LA) Meridonal. "History of Crude Oil as a Useful Tool Told." July 16, 1973.

Afro-American. "Cops War on Voodoo." February 27, 1937.

———. "Hoodoo on Voodoo Dolls Says U.S. Health Service." November 29, 1958.

Alabama Journal (Montgomery). "'Voodoo Woman' Learned Healing Ways as Child." June 15, 1977.

Anniston (AL) Star. "Spirits Haunt Their Victims on Lonely Backroads." June 24, 1990.

Atlanta World. "Voodooism Gets Woman in Jail." March 2, 1932.

Austin-American Statesman. "Colored People Excited." October 27, 1888.

Bishop, Agnes Ware. *Folk-lore or Voodoo.* WPA Alabama Writers Project, Dallas County, 1936.

Buffalo (NY) Courier. "'Black Cat Bone' Order Terrifying Negroes in South." April 18, 1926.

Cazalas, James. "Street that Gave Birth to Blues Is Dying of Old Age." *Delta Democrat Times* (Greenville, MS), March 6, 1965.

Chambers, Douglas B. *Murder in Montpelier: Igbo Africans in Virginia.* Jackson: University Press of Mississippi, 2009.

Charlotte Observer. "Lecture on Africa." February 8, 1880.

Chillicothe (MO) Constitution Tribune. "A Noted Healer." April 13, 1908.

Chillicothe (MO) Morning Constitution. "Casket Too Large for the Hearse." December 10, 1913.

Cincinnati Enquirer. "The Voudou Party." June 1, 1889.

Clarion-Ledger (Jackson, MS). "Aged Man Is Found Dead after Federal Complaint Is Filed." January 24, 1943.

———. "Carried Hoodoo Bags." October 29, 1891.

———. "Clarke Nurse Has Collection of 'Voodoo' Protection Charms." July 30, 1969.

———. "'Elder' Among Last of Old Faithfuls." September 1, 1957.

———. "Hoodoo Dust Fails to Save Negro from Prison." September 6, 1933.

———. "Lincoln Man Bomb Suspect." March 14, 1956.

———. "To Hoodoo a Church Violates What State Law?" October 27, 1954.

———. "Voodoo Doctor Charged." April 28, 1964.

———. "Voodoo Doctors Getting in Way." February 2, 1940.

Commercial Appeal (Memphis, TN). "Hoodoo Plague Rampant: True Story of Darkest Africa as It Exists in Memphis." September 30, 1895.

Courier-Journal (Louisville, KY). "Hoodoo Baby Was Preserved in Alcohol as Luck Token." November 22, 1905.

———. "Hunches and Dreams." May 14, 1950.

Crowder, Steven. "Black Folk Medicine in Southern Appalachia" (master's thesis). East Tennessee State University School of Graduate Studies, 2001.

Daily Arkansas Gazette. "Voodoo Woman Arrested." June 6, 1907.

Daily News (New York). "When Simon Has that Look in His Eyes, Future Unfolds." February 23, 1941.

Daily-News Journal (Murfreesboro, TN). "Bosom Serpent a Rutherford Snake." January 24, 2010.

———. "Negro Surrenders after Talk with Fortune Teller." January 17, 1950.

Delta-Democrat Times (Greenville, MS). "The Astrologer Got in Bad." July 12, 1911.

———. "City Court Fines Root and Voodoo Negro Doctor." January 30, 1940.

———. "Deputy Claims 'Voodoo Medicine' Caused Infection." January 2, 1957.

Democratic Advocate (Westminster, MD). "Items of News." June 21, 1870.

Deslippe, Phillip. "The Hindu in Hoodoo: Fake-Yogis, Pseudo-Swamis, and the Manufacture of African-American Folk Magic." *Amerasia Journal* 40, no. 1 (2014).

Des Moines Tribune. "Explains Mysteries of the Conjure Bag." June 14, 1915.

Diard, Francois Ludgere. *A Superstitious Negro's Hoodoo Murder*. WPA Alabama Writers Project, District 6. Mobile, Alabama, 1936.

Enterprise-Journal (McComb, MS). "Quacks and Hoodoos." April 16, 1940.

———. "'Voodoo Medicine' Claim Disputed by Delta Doctor." January 4, 1957.

Fairleigh, Paul. "Bubble Bubble—But the 'Toil and Trouble' Mostly Bell's." *Press-Scimitar* (Memphis, TN), August 22, 1951.

Fort Lauderdale News. "Testimony Kept from Jury: Voodoo Tried in Hoffa Case." April 29, 1964.

Gadsden (AL) Times. "Crime Doctor Murdered in Voodoo Hex Slaying." March 23, 1957.

Greenwood (MS) Commonwealth. "'Voodoo Doctor' Arrested in Girl's Death." April 27, 1964.

———. "Voodoo Woman Fined to Mississippi Negroes." May 18, 1929.

Gundaker, Grey, and Judith McWillie. *No Space Hidden: The Spirit of African American Yard Work*. Knoxville: University of Tennessee Press, 2005.

Handy, Sara M. "Negro Superstitions." *Lippincott's Monthly Magazine* 48 (1891).

Harris, Garrad. "Plantation Life in Dixie." *Frank Leslie's Popular Monthly* 44 (July–December 1897).

Hattiesburg (MS) American. "Says Students Have Ability to Believe They Will Faint Next." April 11, 1976.

———. "Voodoo It Can Be Had Here." January 14, 1979.

———. "'Voodoo' Preacher in Jail." June 24, 1977.

Hazzard-Donald, Katrina. *Mojo Workin': The Old African American Hoodoo System*. Champaign: University of Illinois, 2012.

Hurdle, Virginia Jo. "Folklore of a Negro Couple in Henry County." *Tennessee Folklore Society Bulletin* 19 (1953).

Jackson, Joyce Marie. "Black Preaching Styles: Teaching, Exhorting and Whooping." Baton Rouge Traditions, Folklife in Louisiana. http://www.louisianafolklife.org/LT/Articles_Essays/brpreaching.html.

Jackson (MS) Daily News. "Plays on Superstition." May 15, 1910.

Jackson (MS) Sun. "'Bishop' Becomes Free Man after Federal Court Hearing." January 12, 1949.

———. "Fifty Years Together." September 3, 1941.

Kentucky Advocate. "Hoodoos." May 7, 1925.

Leaf-Chronicle (Clarksville, TN). "'Bishop St. Psalm' Faces Attempted Extortion Charge," February 20, 1964.

Lindy, Julie. "Absolutely Charming." *Alabama Journal*, January 14, 1985.

Lipscomb, John. "Charms for the Goddess." *Tennessean*, April 3, 1949.

Livingston (AL) Journal. "A Disciple of Hecate." November 5, 1885.

McIlwaine, Shields. "Memphis Down in Dixie." *Colonial Press*, 1948.

McPherson, N.M. "A Question of Morality: Sorcery and Concepts of Deviance among the Kabana, West New Britain." *Anthropologica* 33, nos. 1–2 (1991).

Memphis Daily-Appeal. "Africa. A Missionary from the West Coast of Africa—Rev. W.W. Culley Lectures at the Beale Street Baptist Church." October 15, 1880.

———. "Attempted Poisoning of a Family, the Plot Frustrated." July 15, 1868.

———. "Colored Curiosities: The Prevalence of Hoodooism Among the Blacks." June 30, 1871.

Mississippi: A Guide to the Magnolia State. Works Progress Administration. Washington, D.C., 1938.

Montgomery (AL) Advertiser. "Corpse of the Kudzu Is Alive on Ghost Road." October 30, 1973.

———. "Doctor Refutes Negro 'Voodoo' Wounds." January 4, 1957.

———. "Negro Clings to Ancient Superstitions Just as He Did Half a Century Ago." December 2, 1917.

———. "Negroe's Tale of Jail Beating in Jackson Spurs Probe Appeal." January 3, 1957.

———. "Negro Thief Held as Death Suspect." March 26, 1938.

———. "New Orleans Voodoo Doctor's Practitioner Is Arrested Here." October 23, 1941.

Mynders, Alfred. "The Numbers Game." *Alabama Journal*, March 2, 1944.

Natchez (LA) Democrat. "Forty Years of Freedom." November 18, 1906.

New Journal and Guide (Norfolk, VA). "Man Shoots Wife on 'Voodoo' Charge." June 9, 1943.

Olsen, Ted, and Anthony Cavender. *A Tennessee Folklore Sampler: Selected Readings from the Tennessee Folklore Society Bulletin.* Knoxville: University of Tennessee Press, 2009.

"Original Sixth and Seventh Books of Moses" (advertisement). *Our Southern Home*, August 29, 1923.

Ownby, Ted, and Reagan Wilson. *The Mississippi Encyclopedia.* Jackson: University Press of Mississippi, 2017.

Parr, Jerry S. "Folk Cures of Middle Tennessee." *Tennessee Folklore Society Bulletin* 28, nos. 8–12 (1962).

Parsons, Mildred. "Negro Folklore from Fayette County." *Tennessee Folklore Society Bulletin* 19 (1953).

Philadelphia Tribune. "Bagful of Brimstone Told Gold Diggers Where to Dig." February 6, 1954.

Pine Bluff (AR) Daily Graphic. "A Voodoo Doctor Causes the Death of an Old Colored Woman at Pastoria." May 20, 1896.

Pittsburg Courier. "Had Power to Cure Erring Couples, Held." December 20, 1924.

———. "Hold Doctor in Mail Fraud." June 23, 1937.

———. "117 Tell Court His Medicine Cured 'Em." May 21, 1938.

Puckett, Newbell Niles. *Folk Beliefs of the Southern Negro*. Chapel Hill: University of North Carolina Press, 1926.

Randolph, Paschal Beverly. *Eulis! The History of Love: Its Wondrous Magic, Chemistry, Rules, Laws, Modes, Moods and Rationale*. Boston: Randolph Publishing, 1896.

Repository (Canton, OH). "Monday After: Novelty Dolls Determined to Be a Health Hazard." Cantonrep.com. December 12, 2008.

Rice, Kym S., and Martha B. Katz-Hyman. *World of a Slave: Encyclopedia of the Material Life of Slaves in the United States*. Westport, CT: Greenwood, 2010.

Richmond (VA) Dispatch. "A Voudou Dance." November 14, 1857.

Rollings, Lynn. "Medicine Man." *Alabama Journal*, October 30, 1987.

Sea Coast Echo (Bay St. Louis, MS). "Devil Worship Still Exists." April 13, 1918.

Solinski, Ted. "Fortune Teller Shot to Death in Shelbyville." *Tennessean*, March 23, 1957.

St. Louis Star and Times. "Hoodoo Charges against Negro Girl Are Ruled Out." August 26, 1937.

Tennessean. "Black Shadows of Congo Gods Hover Snug Cottage in New Orleans." July 2, 1930.

———. "Curse Remains on Seer Killer." March 24, 1957.

———. "'Divine Healer' Arrested." August 23, 1959.

———. "Dr. W.M. McLane Indian & German Root Doctor." August 24, 1853.

———. "Guilty Conscience." November 18, 1908.

———. "Hindu Hoodoo, 19, Cuts Negro Wife 222 Times; She Lives." May 24, 1925.

———. "Is It a Hoodoo Charm? Blind Woman Selling Amulet to Nashville Gamblers." May 27, 1896.

———. "Lemon Formula 'Hoodoo' Doctor Sold Wife Sours Roscoe, So He Seeks Help from Law." August 18, 1934.

———. "Lord Forbids Brewing, Bishop Says." January 28, 1963.
———. "Seer of Shelbyville, Bill Holder." May 11, 1947.
Times-Democrat (New Orleans, LA). "Conquers the Devil." May 21, 1902.
———. "Fake Fakir: So Called 'Dr. Koku' Exposed by a Committee." May 24, 1902.
———. "Koku, the Strenuous." May 22, 1902.
Town Talk (Alexandria, LA). "Superstition Being Fought in the War on Syphilis." February 2, 1940.
U.S. Department of Agriculture. Notices of Judgment Under the Federal Food, Drug, and Cosmetic Act. Drugs and Devices. Issues 1–2670. Washington, D.C. 1949.
Vicksburg (MS) Herald. "Killed a Hoodoo Doctor." April 16, 1901.
Wallach, Jennifer Jensen. *Dethroning the Deceitful Pork Chop: Rethinking African American Foodways from Slavery to Obama*. Fayetteville: University of Arkansas Press, 2015.
Washington Times. "Red 'Conjure Bag' President's Jinx for Rheumatism." February 28, 1919.
Weekly Democrat (Natchez, MS). "Doctress Emily Gibson." June 7, 1869.
Weekly Messenger (St. Martinsville, LA). "Proved Oil Territory for Development." May 15, 1915.
Whitten, Norman E. "Contemporary Patterns of Malign Occultism among Negroes in North Carolina." *Journal of American Folklore* 75, no. 298 (1962): 311–25.
Williams, Nat D. "Down on Beale." *Pittsburg Courier*, February 4, 1950.
Wood, Betty. *Slavery in Colonial America 1619–1776*. Lanham, MD: Rowman & Littlefield, 2005.

ABOUT THE AUTHOR

Tony Kail is a cultural anthropologist, ethnographer and writer. Kail holds a degree in cultural anthropology and has been involved in research of magico-religious cultures for more than twenty-five years. His work has taken him from Vodou ceremonies in New Orleans to Haitian Botanicas in Harlem and Spirit churches in East Africa. He is a cultural consultant for local, state and federal medical and public safety agencies on issues related to cultural diversity, religious culture and transcultural communication. He has lectured at more than one hundred universities, hospitals and public safety agencies throughout the United States. He has been featured on CNN Online, the History Channel and numerous radio, television and print outlets. He is the author of ten books, including *A Secret History of Memphis Hoodoo: Rootworkers, Conjurers and Spirituals* from The History Press and *Art of the Conjure: Curios and Curiosities of Southern Hoodoo Culture* from John the Conqueror Press.